A Song Flung Up to Heaven

A
Song
Flung Up
to Heaven

MAYA ANGELOU

BANTAM BOOKS

NEW YORK   TORONTO   LONDON   SYDNEY   AUCKLAND

A SONG FLUNG UP TO HEAVEN
A Bantam Book

PUBLISHING HISTORY
Random House hardcover edition published April 2002
Bantam trade paperback edition / April 2003

Published by Bantam Dell
A Division of Random House, Inc.
New York, New York

Book design by Carole Lowenstein

Library of Congress Catalog Card Number: 2001034914

Bantam Books and the rooster colophon are registered
trademarks of Random House, Inc.

ISBN 0-553-38203-9

Manufactured in the United States of America
Published simultaneously in Canada

RRH   10 9 8 7 6 5 4 3 2 1

Dedicated to
Caylin Nicole Johnson
Brandon Bailey Johnson
and to my entire family
wherever and whoever
you are

Acknowledgments

I thank seven of my living teachers:

The Reverends

Frederick Buechner
Eric Butterworth
Serenus T. Churn, Sr.
H. Beecher Hicks
Barbara King
Cecil Williams
Andrew Young

A Song Flung Up to Heaven

One

The old ark's a-movering
a-movering
a-movering
the old ark's a-movering
and I'm going home.

—*Nineteenth-century American spiritual*

The old ark was a Pan Am jet and I was returning to the United States. The airplane had originated in Johannesburg and stopped in Accra, Ghana, to pick up passengers.

I boarded, wearing traditional West African dress, and sensed myself immediately, and for the first time in years, out of place. A presentiment of unease enveloped me before I could find my seat at the rear of the plane. For the first few minutes I busied myself arranging bags, souvenirs, presents. When I finally settled into my narrow seat, I looked around and became at once aware of the source of my discomfort. I was among more white people than I had seen in four years. During that period I had not once thought of not seeing white people; there were European, Canadian and white American faculty at the university where I worked. Roger and Jean Genoud, who were Swiss United Nations personnel, had become my close friends and in fact helped me to raise—or better, corral—my teenage son. So my upset did not come from seeing the white complexion, but rather, from seeing so much of it at one time.

For the next seven hours, I considered the life I was leaving and the circumstances to which I was returning. I thought of the difference between the faces I had just embraced in farewell and those on the plane who looked at me and other blacks who also boarded in Accra with distaste, if not outright disgust. I thought of my rambunctious nineteen-year-old son, whom I was leaving with a family of Ghanaian friends. I also left him under the watchful eye and, I hoped, tender care of God, who seemed to be the only force capable of controlling him.

My thoughts included the political climate I was leaving. It was a known fact that antigovernment forces were aligning themselves at that very moment to bring down the regime of Kwame Nkrumah, Ghana's controversial, much adored but also much hated president. The atmosphere was thick with accusations, threats, fear, guilt, greed and capriciousness. Yet at least all the visible participants in that crowded ambience were black, in contrast to the population in the environment to which I was returning. I knew that the air in the United States was no less turbulent than that in Ghana. If my mail and the world newspapers were to be believed, the country was clamoring with riots and pandemonium. The cry of "burn, baby, burn" was loud in the land, and black people had gone from the earlier mode of "sit-in" to "set fire," and from "march-in" to "break-in."

Malcolm X, on his last visit to Accra, had announced a desire to create a foundation he called the Organization of African-American Unity. His proposal included taking the plight of the African-Americans to the United Nations and asking the world council to intercede on the part of beleaguered blacks. The idea was so stimulating to the community of African-American residents that I persuaded myself I should return to the States to help establish the organization. Alice Windom and Vickie Garvin, Sylvia Boone and Julian Mayfield, African-Americans who lived and worked in Ghana, were also immediate supporters. When I informed them that I had started making plans to go back to America to work with Malcolm, they—my friends, buddies, pals—began to treat me as if I had suddenly become special. They didn't speak quite so loudly around me, they didn't clap my back when laughing; nor were they as quick to point out my flaws. My stature had definitely increased.

We all read Malcolm's last letter to me.

Dear Maya,

I was shocked and surprised when your letter arrived but I was also pleased because I only had to wait two months for this one whereas previously I had to wait almost a year. You see I haven't lost my wit. (smile)

Your analysis of our people's tendency to talk over the head of the masses in a language that is too far above and beyond them is certainly true. You can communicate because you have plenty of (soul) and you always keep your feet firmly rooted on the ground.

I am enclosing some articles that will give you somewhat of an idea of my daily experiences here and you will then be better able to understand why it sometimes takes me a long time to write. I was most pleased to learn that you might be hitting in this direction this year. You are a

*beautiful writer and a beautiful woman. You know that I
will always do my utmost to be helpful to you in any way
possible so don't hesitate.*

Signed

Your brother Malcolm

I looked around the plane at the South African faces
and thought of Vus Make, my latest husband, from whom
I had separated. He and members of the Pan-African
Congress and Oliver Tambo, second in command of the
African National Congress, really believed they would be
able to change the hearts and thereby the actions of the
apartheid-loving Boers. In the early sixties I called them
Nation Dreamers. When I thought of Robert Sobukwe,
leader of the Pan-African Congress who had languished
for years in prison, and Nelson Mandela, who had
recently been arrested, I was sure that they would spend
their lives sealed away from the world. I had thought that,
despite their passion and the rightness of their cause, the
two men would become footnotes on the pages of history.

Now, with the new developments about to take place,
I felt a little sympathy for the Boers, and congratulated
myself and all African-Americans for our courage. The

passion my people would exhibit under Malcolm's leadership was going to help us rid our country of racism once and for all. The Africans in South Africa often said they had been inspired by Martin Luther King, Jr., and the Montgomery bus boycott of 1958. Well, we were going to give them something new, something visionary, to look up to. After we had cleansed ourselves and our country of hate, they would be able to study our methods, take heart from our example and let freedom ring in their country as it would ring in ours.

Sweet dreams of the future blunted the sharp pain of leaving both my son and the other important man in my life. Given enough time, Guy would eventually grow up and be a fine man, but my romantic other could never fit into my world, nor I into his.

He was a powerful West African who had swept into my life with the urgency of a Southern hurricane. He uprooted my well-planted ideas and blew down all my firmly held beliefs about decorum.

I had been in love many times before I met him, but I had never surrendered myself to anyone. I had given my word and my body, but I had never given my soul. The African had the habit of being obeyed, and he insisted on having all of me. The pleasure I found with him made me unable, or at least unwilling, to refuse.

Within a month of conceding my authority over myself and my life to another, I realized the enormity of my mistake. If I wanted chicken, he said he wanted lamb, and I quickly agreed. If I wanted rice, he wanted yams, and I quickly agreed. He said that I was to go along with whatever he wanted, and I agreed. If I wanted to visit with my friends and he wanted to be alone but not without me, I agreed.

I began to feel the pinch of his close embrace the first time I wanted to sit up and read and he wanted to go to bed.

And, he added, I was needed.

I agreed.

But I thought, "Needed?" Needed like an extra blanket? Like air-conditioning? Like more pepper in the soup? I resented being thought of as a thing, but I had to admit that I allowed the situation myself and had no reason to be displeased with anyone save myself.

Each time I gave up my chicken for his lamb, I ate less. When I gave up a visit with friends to stay home with him, I enjoyed him less. And when I joined him, leaving my book abandoned on the desk, I found I had less appetite for the bedroom.

"You Americans can be bullheaded, stupid and crazy. Why would you kill President Kennedy?" He didn't hear me say, "I didn't kill the president."

My return to the United States came at the most opportune time. I could leave my son to his manly development hurdles; I would leave my great, all-consuming love to his obedient subjects; and I would return to work with Malcolm X on building the Organization of African-American Unity.

By the time we arrived in New York, I had discarded my vilification of the white racists on the plane and had even begun to feel a little more sorry for them.

I was saddened by their infantile, puerile minds. They could be assured that as soon as we American blacks got our country straight, the Xhosas, Zulus, Matabeles, Shonas and others in southern Africa would lead their whites from the gloom of ignorance into the dazzling light of understanding.

The sound in the airport was startling. The open air in Africa was often loud, with many languages being spoken at once, children crying, drums pounding—that had been noise, but at New York's Idlewild Airport, the din that aggressively penetrated the air, insisting on being heard, was clamor. There were shouts and orders, screams, implorings and demands, horns blaring and voices booming. I found a place beside a wall and leaned against it. I had been away from the cacophony for four years, but now I was home.

After I gathered my senses, I found a telephone booth.

I knew I was not ready for New York's strenuous energy, but I needed to explain that to my New York friends. I had written Rosa Guy, my supportive sister-friend, and she was expecting me. I also needed to call Abbey Lincoln, the jazz singer, and her husband, Max Roach, the jazz drummer, who had offered me a room in their Columbus Avenue apartment that I had refused. But most especially, I had to speak to Malcolm.

His telephone voice caught me off guard. I realized I had never spoken to him on the telephone.

"Maya, so you finally got here. How was the trip?" His voice was higher-pitched than I expected.

"Fine."

"You stay at the airport, I'll be there to pick you up. I'll leave right now."

I interrupted. "I'm going straight to San Francisco. My plane leaves soon."

"I thought you were coming to work with us in New York."

"I'll be back in a month . . ." I explained that I needed to be with my mother and my brother, Bailey, just to get used to being back in the United States.

Malcolm said, "I had to leave my car in the Holland Tunnel. Somebody was trying to get me. I jumped in a white man's car. He panicked. I told him who I was, and he said, 'Get down low, I'll get you out of this.' You believe that, Maya?"

I said yes, but I found it hard to do so. "I'll call you next week when I get my bearings."

Malcolm said, "Well, let me tell you about Betty and the girls." I immediately remembered the long nights in Ghana when our group sat and listened to him talk about the struggle, racism, political strategies and social unrest. Then he would speak of Betty. His voice would soften and take on a new melody. We would be told of her great intelligence, of her beauty, of her wit. How funny she was and how faithful. We would hear that she was an adoring mother and a brave and loving wife.

Malcolm said, "She is here now and making a wonderful dinner. You know she is pretty and pregnant. Pretty pregnant." He laughed at his own joke.

I said, "Please give her my regards. I must run for my plane. I'll call you next week."

"Do that. Safe trip."

I hurriedly telephoned Max Roach and Abbey Lincoln to say that I was home. They also offered to pick me up from the airport, but I told them I would phone them next week from San Francisco.

Rosa Guy listened to my explanation and understood. Our conversation was brief.

I thought of calling James Baldwin, who had become a close friend. We met in Paris in the 1950s when he was writing and I was the principal dancer in the opera *Porgy and Bess*. We became closer in 1960 when I lived in New York. Jimmy was familiar with the work of Jean Genet, and when I played the White Queen in the Genet drama

The Blacks, he spent long evenings helping me with the role. I didn't telephone him because I knew he could persuade me to stay in New York for at least a day. His physical smallness, his sense of humor and his love for me reminded me so much of my brother, Bailey, that I could never completely resist him.

Two

My mother met me at the San Francisco airport. She was smaller and prettier than she had been in my memory. She kissed me and said, "Describe your luggage to the skycaps, they will bring your bags to the car." The porters had eyes only for my mother. They danced attendance on her, like a male corps de ballet around the première danseuse, and she didn't even seem to notice. Mother rushed us to the car and my heart leaped to find Bailey sitting in the backseat. He had flown in from Hawaii to meet me and at once began talking and asking questions.

Mother said, "She grew prettier. You're a good-looking woman, baby."

Bailey said, "Yeah, but good looks run in this family. She didn't have anything to do with that. Tell me about Guy."

Mother said, "I read in the papers that you were coming back to work with Malcolm X in some new organization. I hope not. I really hope not." She paused and then continued, "If you feel you have to do that—work for no money—go back to Martin Luther King. He's really trying to help our people. Malcolm X is a rabble-rouser."

My breath left me and I couldn't seem to get it back. Just as suddenly, I had enough air, and as I opened my mouth to respond, Bailey touched my shoulder and I turned to him. His face was solemn as he wagged his head. I closed my mouth.

Although less than two years older than I and barely five feet four, my brother had been my counselor and protector for as long as I could remember. When we were just three and five, our parents separated. They sent us, unaccompanied, from California to our paternal grandmother and uncle, who lived in Stamps, a small Arkansas hamlet. Since the adults were strangers to us, Bailey became head of a family that consisted of just us two. He was quicker to learn than I, and he took over teaching me what to do and how to do it.

When I was seven, our handsome, dapper California father arrived in the dusty town. After dazzling the country folk, including his mother, his brother and his children, he took Bailey and me to St. Louis to live with our mother, who had moved back to Missouri after their divorce. He wasn't concerned with offering us a better life, but rather, with curtailing the life my mother was living as a pretty woman who was single again.

My grandmother bundled us and a shoe box of fried chicken into my father's car and cried as she waved good-bye. My father drove, hardly stopping until he delivered us to my mother in St. Louis.

For the first few months we were enraptured with the exotic Northern family. Our maternal grandmother looked white and had a German accent. Our grandfather was black and spoke with a Trinidadian accent. Their four sons swaggered into and out of their house like movie toughs.

Their food astonished us. They ate liverwurst and salami, which we had never seen. Their sliced bread was white and came in greasy, slick waxed paper, and after eating only homemade ice cream, we thought there could be nothing greater than enjoying slices of multicolored cold slabs cut from a brick of frozen dessert. We delighted in being big-city kids until my mother's boyfriend raped me. After much persuasion (the man had warned me that if I told anyone, he would kill my brother), I told Bailey, who told the family. The man was arrested, spent one night in jail, was released and found dead three days later.

The police who informed my grandmother of the man's death, in front of me, said it seemed he had been kicked to death.

The account staggered me. I thought my voice had killed the man, so I stopped speaking and Bailey became my shadow, as if he and I were playing a game. If I turned left, he turned left; if I sat, he sat. He hardly let me out of his sight. The large, rambunctious big-city family tried to woo me out of my stolid silence, but when I stubbornly refused to talk, Bailey and I were both sent back to Arkansas. For the next six years, my brother was the only person for whom I would bring my voice out of concealment. I thought my voice was such poison that it could kill anyone. I spoke to him only rarely and sometimes incomprehensibly, but I felt that because I loved him so much, my voice might not harm him.

In our early teens we returned to our mother, who had moved back to California. Our lives began to differ. Just as Bailey had shadowed me earlier, he now seemed set on opposing each move I made. If I went to school, he cut class. If I refused narcotics, he wanted to experiment. If I stayed home, he became a merchant marine. Yet despite our dissimilar routes and practices, I never lost my complete trust in Bailey.

And now, as I sat in my mother's car being bombarded by the metropolitan flash and my mother's attack on Malcolm, I held my peace; Bailey encouraged me to do so, and I knew he would be proven right.

My mother's Victorian house on Fulton Street was exactly as it had been when I left four years earlier. She had bought new rugs and added or changed some furniture, but the light still entered the tall windows boldly, and the air still held the dual scent of Tweed perfume and a slight hint of gas escaping from a very small aperture.

I was encouraged to put my bags in my old bedroom and then to join Mother and Bailey in the vast kitchen for a sumptuous welcome-home.

Mother told racy stories, and Bailey regaled me with Hawaiian songs and then gave me his interpretation of an island man's hula. Mother brought out a recipe for Jollof rice that I had sent her from Ghana. She unfolded the letter and read, "Cook about a pound of rice, sauté a couple or three onions in not too much cooking oil for a while, then put in three or four or five right-sized tomatoes . . ."

At this point in her recitation, Bailey began laughing. He was a professional chef in a swank Hawaiian hotel. The approximation of ingredients and cooking time amused him.

"Dice some cooked ham in fairly large-sized pieces," my mother continued, "and include with salt and cayenne pepper any leftover fried chicken into the tomato sauce. Heat through, then mix in with rice. Then heat quite a while."

We all laughed when Mother said she had followed the recipe exactly and that the dish was a smashing success.

Bailey then told us stories about the tourists and their dining orders at his Waikiki hotel: "I'd like fried chicken and biscuits." "Y'all have any short ribs and corn bread?"

Mother telephoned friends, who dropped by to look at me and Bailey. Many spoke of us as if we weren't in the room.

"Vivian, she looks so good. I know you're proud." And "Well, Bailey didn't grow any more, but he sure is a pretty little black thing."

The entire weekend was a riot of laughter, stories, memories awakened and relished in the bright sunlight. The specter of my distant son cast the only shadow. His arrogance and intractability were discussed, and my family put his behavior in its proper place.

My mother said, "He's a boy."

I said, "He thinks he is a man." Mother said, "That's the nature of the group. When they are boys, they want to be treated like men, but when they are gray-haired old coots, they go around acting like boys." No one could argue with that. "Don't worry about him. You have raised him with love. The fruit won't fall too far from the tree."

The finality in her tone told me she was finished with the subject, but I wondered—what if the fruit fell and was picked up by a hungry bird? Wasn't it possible that it could end up on a dung heap far away from the mother tree?

These were the bleak moments in my homecoming that could not be brightened by Bailey's quick wit or my mother's hilarious homilies.

I had been a journalist in Cairo, and Guy had finished high school there. We moved to Ghana, and when he recovered from a devastating automobile accident, he entered the university. Classrooms were not large enough to hold all of him. When I talked to him about the importance of grades, he patted my head and said, "I understand your interest, little Mother, but those are my concerns and my business. I'll take care of them."

For two years, Guy weaned himself away from my nurture. He broke dates with me, and when I surprised him with an unannounced visit, he firmly let me know that I was not welcome.

When I chose to return to the U.S. to work with Malcolm, I paid Guy's tuition through his graduating year. I told him he could have all the freedom he required. In fact, I said I would give him Ghana.

The paramount chief Nana Nketsi IV assured me that he would pay sharp attention to Guy; and the Genouds, who were childless, assured me that Guy would be like a son to them. They promised to give me a monthly report on how he was faring, so I should feel at ease.

Of course I didn't. From the moment I bought my ticket, guilt called out my name.

Guy was nineteen, and I, who had been his shade since he was born, was leaving him under the broiling African sun. Each time I would try to speak with him about his future, he would cut me off. When I tried to talk about my departure, he curtly told me that indeed I should go home, to go and work with Malcolm. Guy was a man who was trying to live his own life.

Three

The golden morning was definitely a San Francisco Sunday. I dressed quickly and left the house. I had been home less than forty-eight hours, and already I had a creeping sensation that I should be moving on. My mother was comfortably encircled by her ring of friends, and Bailey, who had shown me on Friday night how Hawaiian men enjoyed themselves, and on Saturday night how San Franciscans still did their weekend partying, was planning to return the next week to the Hawaiian Islands.

The streets were empty. San Franciscans who hadn't gone to church were sleeping off Saturday-night parties. I walked through parks and trudged up hills. At every peak, I was struck by the beauty that lay invitingly at the foot of the hill.

I had not consciously considered a destination, but I found myself at the end of Golden Gate Park's panhandle, and I realized that my mother's close friend lived nearby.

Aunt Lottie Wells had come to San Francisco from Los Angeles ten years earlier. She joined the family, became my friend and helped me to raise Guy. Her house was a smaller version of Mother's home. Fresh-cut flowers were everywhere, reposing on highly polished tables beneath glistening mirrors.

She said she knew I would visit her, so she hadn't gone to church. She had a pan of biscuits in the oven and was ready to fold over one of her light-as-air omelettes. Lottie smiled, and I was glad that the spirit of wanderers, which lived with me, had brought me to her home.

Her telephone rang as we were sitting down to the table. She answered it in the hall.

She returned. "It's Ivonne for you," she said, grinning. "She called your house and your mother told her you would probably stop by here."

Ivonne was my first adult friend, and I knew we would spend some delicious hours talking about ourselves, the men we loved and the ones who got away. We had never been slow to give each other advice, although I didn't remember either of us being quick to hearken to the other's counsel.

I picked up the phone. "Hey, girl. Where are you? How are you doing?"

"Maya, girl, why did you come home? Why did you come back to this crazy place?"

There was no cheer in her voice.

"I came back because I think I have something to do."

She said, "These Negroes are crazy here. I mean, really crazy. Otherwise, why would they have just killed that man in New York?"

I took the phone away from my ear and looked at it. I cradled it in my hands, looking at its dull black surface; then I laid it down on the hall table. Instead of returning to the dining room, I walked into a bedroom and locked the door.

I didn't have to ask. I knew "that man in New York" was Malcolm X and that someone had just killed him.

Four

Bailey's anxious voice awakened me.

"My. My. Open this door. Open it now."

At times when my life has been ripped apart, when my feet forget their purpose and my tongue is no longer familiar with the inside of my mouth, a touch of narcolepsy has befriended me. I have fallen asleep as an adored lover told me that his fancy had flown. When my son was severely injured in the automobile crash, I couldn't eat and could barely talk, but I could fall asleep sitting on the straight-back metal hospital chairs beside his door.

This time I woke up in a strange room knowing everything. I was still in Aunt Lottie's house, and Malcolm was dead. I had returned from Africa to give my energies and wit to the OAAU, and Malcolm was dead.

"Open this door, My. Wake up and open the damn door or I'll break it down."

He would. I turned the lock.

He looked at my face. "I'm sorry, baby. Go in the bathroom and wash up. I'm taking you somewhere. Somewhere important. Go on."

My bloated face and swollen eyes told me I had cried, but I didn't remember and didn't want to remember.

Bailey waited in the hall, holding my purse and jacket.

"Here, take this. Put this on. Say good–bye to Aunt Lottie."

She took me in her arms. "So sorry, baby. So sorry."

My eyesight and my equilibrium failed me, so Bailey guided me down the hills. He always knew when and when not to talk. He remained silent as we walked out of the residential district and on to the Fillmore area. There, all the people who had been absent from the streets earlier were now very much present, but in ordinary ways. Shouts, conversation and laughter seemed to cascade out of every door. Customers left and entered grocery stores, absorbed in conversation. Men stood in front of saloons engaged in dialogue so private it needed to be whispered. I was shocked to see life going on as usual.

I said to Bailey, "They don't know."

Bailey grunted. "They know. They don't care."

"What do you mean they don't care? I can't accept that. When they know that Malcolm has been killed, the people will riot. They'll explode."

Bailey deftly steered me through the open door of the smoky Havana Bar, where the jukebox music vied with customers' voices.

I looked into the grinning faces and was stumped. In Ghana, I had read that the mood of unrest here was so great that the black community was like a powder keg that would take very little to detonate. But only hours after their champion had been killed, black men and women were flirting and drinking and reveling as if nothing had happened. Bailey ordered two drinks, and when the bartender slid them in front of us, my brother touched me with his elbow and asked the bartender, "Hey, man, you hear what happened to Malcolm X?"

The bartender made a swiping gesture with the bill Bailey had laid down.

"Well, hell, man. They shot him. You know they say, you live by the sword, you die by the sword."

He added ignorance to ignorance by pronouncing the "sw" in sword like the "sw" in the word "swear."

"How dare you . . . don't you know what Malcolm X has done?"

Bailey took my arm. "Thanks, man. Keep the change."

In seconds I was outside in the clear air, and Bailey was propelling me along Fillmore Street.

"Come on. We're going to Jack's Tavern."

That historic saloon had been my mother's hangout for years. The clientele tended to be older, more established, more professional. They would know the importance of Malcolm's life and most certainly the importance of his death. I needed to be there quickly, so I began to walk a little faster.

Bailey said, "Don't set yourself up to be knocked down. Keep your expectations in control."

The night before, I had told him of my disappointment with Mother. She didn't appreciate or even understand Malcolm and the struggle of black people for equality.

I asked, "Does she think she's liberated?"

Bailey said, as if he had always known it, "Some folks say they want change. They just want exchange. They only want to have what the haves have, so they won't have it anymore. Now, Mom is not like that. She just wants to be left alone. She thinks if no one gets in her way, she can get her freedom by herself. She doesn't want even Martin Luther King to tell her where her liberation lies—and certainly not Malcolm X."

When we walked into Jack's Tavern, we were greeted by Mother's friends.

"Well, Vivian's children came from the ends of the earth to see about their old mother."

Another voice came from near the bar: "Better not let Vivian hear you call her old."

Someone answered, "If anybody tells her I said it, I'll deny it to my dying day."

"How are you all doing?"

One of the oldest regulars told the bartender, "Set them up. Their money's no good in here."

I was relieved to find Trumpet still tending bar. He had been a pal of mine during the lean days when I was studying and teaching dance, trying to raise my son, keep my love affairs intact and live on one grain of rice and a drop of water. We had spent long hours as buddies, talking about the ways of the world.

I said, "Trumpet, I know you heard about Malcolm."

"Naw, baby. When did you come home? Good-looking old tall long-legged girl."

"Trumpet, Malcolm is dead. Somebody shot him."

Trumpet stood up straight. "Really? No, that's awful. Awful news. Sorry to hear that. When did you get home? How was Africa?"

Bailey said to me, "Get your drink. Let's sit down at a table."

I followed him. He must have seen that at the moment, I was quite soberly going mad.

"You know, of course, that you can't go back to New York. With Malcolm dead, there is no OAAU, and you can't start one or restart his on your own. You wouldn't know who to trust. Accusations are going to be flying thick as grits, and that is no place for you."

Bleakness and grief welled up in me, and I started to cry.

Bailey said, "Stop that. What happened to you in Africa? Did you forget? You can't let people see you cry in public. That's like laying your head down on a chopping block in the presence of an executioner.

"Now, you want the black people to rise up and riot. Don't count on it. Nothing's going to happen right away. I mean nothing. But after a while, a white man is going to step on a black woman's toe, and we'll have a civil war again."

I asked, "What can I do? I don't want to go back to Africa. You say don't go to New York. I hate San Francisco right now."

"Come back to Honolulu with me. Aunt Leah is there. You can stay with her for a while."

My mother's only sister was an evangelist in Oahu, and I didn't take much comfort in Bailey's invitation.

"You can go back to singing in nightclubs. A lot of new places have opened since you were last there."

He continued talking, but I stopped listening and began concentrating on regaining my self-control.

"Maya. Maya." He spoke softly, and for the first time his voice was heavy with sympathy. "Baby, let me tell you what's going to happen. In a few years, there are going to be beautiful posters of Malcolm X, and his photographs will be everywhere. The same people who don't give a damn now will lie and say they always supported him. And that very bartender, the one with the sword"—Bailey mispronounced the word as the bartender had done—"he will say, 'Malcolm was a great man. I always knew he was a great man. A race man. A man who loved his people.'"

I looked at my brother, who was always the wisest person I knew, and wondered if he could possibly be wrong this time.

When we returned home Mother had the grace to give me her sympathy.

"I didn't care for his tactics, but nobody should be shot down like a yard dog. I know he was your friend, baby, and I'm sorry. I want you to know I'm sorry he was killed."

It took me two days to reach Ghana by telephone, and when I did, Guy's voice was hardly audible. He spoke through the crackle of international static.

"I hope you'll enjoy Hawaii, Mom. I was sorry about Malcolm." Then he said, "I am very well. I'm doing fine, and school is fine."

What else could or would he say?

"I've been back to the hospital, and I can play football now."

In the automobile crash years earlier, Guy had broken his neck and spent six months in a torso cast. He healed, but I doubted seriously that he had been given medical clearance to play any full-contact sport.

"Yes, Mother, of course I miss you."

He didn't.

"Mom." His voice began to fade, but for the first time I heard my son's true voice. "Mom, I'm really sorry about Malcolm. We held a vigil in Accra . . . Really, really sorry."

Thousands of air miles and millions of Atlantic waves sandwiched my son's voice, and I could no longer hear him, but I was satisfied. We had lived so close together that through his normal teenage bravado and his newly learned air of male superiority, I could translate him into my mother language fluently. Despite the static and the pauses when the line went dead, despite the faintness of his voice and the loud buzzing that never stopped, the call was, for me, a huge success.

I learned from what he said and what he didn't say that he was living the high life, the very high life. In fact, he was glad that he had been invited to the world party and that there was no mother around to give him curfew hours. He was going to school and enjoying the competition and the open forum for debate, because he was always eager for argument. He missed me, but not in the sense that he wished me back in Ghana. He missed me just because I had left a vacuum. He was glad for the opportunity to furnish the vacuum with his own chosen baubles.

Generally, he was happy in his fortified city of youth. And if a cold breeze blew over the ramparts, he had his bravado to keep him warm.

He was sincerely sorry about Malcolm. He was so near the sacred and fearful grail of black manhood that any man of color who faced the threat of life with courage, and intellect, and wit, was his hero. He included among his paladins Mahatma Gandhi, Paul Robeson, Nelson Mandela, Mao Tse-tung, Hannibal, Robert Sobukwe and Martin Luther King, Jr. However, Malcolm X topped the list. Guy himself had lost an ideal, so he felt sincere sympathy for me. He knew I had lost a friend.

Five

The San Francisco streets bore out Bailey's predictions. Life was so mundane that I was plunged into despair.

Why were black people so indifferent? Were we unfeeling? Or were we so timid that we were afraid to honor our dead? I thought what a pathetic people we were.

American blacks were acting as if they believed "A man lived, a man loved, a man tried, a man died," and that was all there was to that.

Papers ran pictures of the handsome Malcolm before the assassination alongside the photo of his bloody body, with his wife, Betty, leaning over her beloved on her knees, frozen in shock.

If a group of racists had waylaid Malcolm, killed him in the dark and left his body as a mockery to all black people, I might have accepted his death more easily. But he was killed by black people as he spoke to black people about a better future for black people and in the presence of his family.

Bailey rescued me. He had returned to Hawaii and found a nightclub that was offering me a job singing. He had lined up a rhythm section and had talked Aunt Leah into letting me stay with her until I could find a place.

Mother admitted, "Yes, I phoned your brother. You were prowling around the streets and the house like a lame leopard. Time for you to straighten up and get back into the whirl of life."

She lived life as if it had been created just for her. She thought the only people who didn't feel the same were laggards and layabouts.

One would have to be a determined malcontent to resist her sincere good humor. She played music, cooked wonderful menus of my favorite foods and told me bawdy jokes, partly to entertain and partly to shock me out of my lethargy. Her tactics worked.

We packed for Hawaii with great joviality. Mother bought me beautiful expensive Western clothes. I began to look forward to the trip. With her powerful personality, she had pulled me out of the drowning depths and onto a safe shore. I had not forgotten Malcolm, nor was I totally at ease about Guy, but some of my own good humor had returned, and I was ready to search for a path back into life.

Six

The exterior of Aunt Leah's house was middle–class Southern California ranch–style stucco. The inside was working–class anywhere. A large, light beige sofa and matching chair were dressed in fitted, heavy plastic covers; a curved blond cocktail table bore up a crouching ceramic black panther. The drapes, which remained closed during my entire stay, were a strong defense against the persistent Hawaiian sunlight. Well–worn Bibles lay on all surfaces, and pictures of Jesus hung on all the walls. Some images were of the Saviour looking benignly out of the drawing, and others were the tortured visages of Him upon the cross.

Having spent a month in my mother's tuneful and

colorful house, I felt that I had left reality and entered surreality.

My aunt was religious, and she lived her religion. Her response to "Good morning, how are you?" was "Blessed in the Lord, and Him dead and crucified."

Her husband, named Al but called "Brother"—tradition dictated that I call him "Uncle Brother"—was a big, good-looking country man who adored his wife. He had come from the Arkansas Ozarks with the strength of John Henry, a sunny disposition and very little education. He was working as a laborer when he and my aunt met. She encouraged him to return to school and helped him with his books. By the time they moved to Hawaii, he had become a general contractor who could read a sextant and was building high-rise hotels.

His presence made the house bearable because he didn't take anything too seriously, even my aunt. There was always a shimmer in his eyes when he looked at her: "Yes, baby. Yes, baby, I thanked the Lord, too, but I know the Lord is not going to lay one brick for me. He is not going to plaster one wall. He's counting on me to do that for Him. So I got to go."

Seven

There is reliable verity in the assurance that once one has learned to ride a bicycle, the knowledge never disappears. I could add that this is also true for nightclub singing.

Rehearsing with a rhythm section, putting on a fancy, shiny dress and makeup and stepping up to the microphone was as familiar to me as combing my hair. To my surprise, I remembered how to step gracefully out of a song after I had blundered into it in the wrong key, and how to keep an audience interested even when the tune was a folk song with thirty-nine verses.

Within a few weeks at the Encore in Hawaii, I was

drawing a good crowd that was eager to hear my style of singing calypso songs in a pseudo-African accent.

The love songs of the Gershwins and Duke Ellington and the clever calypso lyrics were my reliable repertoire. I sang to drum, bass and piano accompaniment, and in each set I included one African song that I translated so loosely the original composer would not have recognized it.

The club orchestra played Hawaiian music, which pleased sailors, businessmen and families. They not only enjoyed the music, they joined in on the audience-participation numbers and would sally forth to the dance floor and treat themselves and the establishment to a hula, samba, rumba, jitterbug, cha-cha or even a tap dance.

I would go home to Aunt Leah's around three A.M., and the sensation was as if I had just left Times Square and stepped onto the dock of the bay at the back of the moon.

Auntie didn't believe in much volume, so music from her radios was hardly audible; every now and again the name of Jesus could be heard from a broadcast sermon. Nor did she approve of air-conditioning. Uncle Brother had installed first-rate units in the house, but Aunt Leah was Calvinistic. She was certain that too many physical comforts in this life would cut down on benefits for the Christians lucky enough to get into heaven, or might even make it too difficult to get in at all. The house was dark, and the air was heavy and stayed in one place. With its sluggish mood, it should have been an ideal location in which to indulge a hearty dose of self-pity. But somehow, piety had claimed every inch of air in that house.

Gloom definitely could not find a niche at the night-club. It was impossible to think about the life Guy might be living, or Malcolm's death, or the end of yet another of my marriages made in heaven while I was onstage singing "Stone Cold Dead in the Market" or the Andrews Sisters' irresistible song "Drinking Rum and Coca-Cola."

Offstage, the other entertainers were so busy flirting outrageously, fondling one another or carrying arguments to high-pitched and bitter ends that there was no room in which I could consider my present and my past.

I wanted a place where I could languish. I found a furnished flat, moved in, seated myself, laced my fingers and put my hands in my lap and waited. I expected a litany of pitiful accounts to come to mind, a series of sad tales. I was a woman alone, unable to get a man, and if I got one, I could not hold on to him; I had only one child (West Africans say one child is no child, for if a tragedy befalls him, there is nothing left), and he was beyond my reach in too many ways. I expected a face full of sorry and a lap full of if-you-please. Nothing happened. I didn't get a catch in my throat, and there was no moisture around my eyes.

Didn't I care that I had been a bad mother, abandoning my son, leaving him with a meager bank account and up to his own silly teenage devices? He'd go through that money like Grant went through Richmond, and then what? I thought I should be crying. Not one tear fell.

A kind of stoicism had to have been in my inheritance. My inability to feel enough self-pity to break down and cry did not come from an insensitivity to the situation but rather, from the knowledge that as bad as things are now, they could have been worse and might become worser and even worserer. As had happened so many times in my life, I had to follow my grandmother's teaching.

"Sister, change everything you don't like about your life. But when you come to a thing you can't change, then change the way you think about it. You'll see it new, and maybe a new way to change it."

The African-American leaves the womb with the burden of her color and a race memory chockablock with horrific folk tales. Frequently there are songs, toe-tapping, finger-popping, hand-slapping, dancing songs that say, in effect, "I'm laughing to keep from crying." Gospel, blues and love songs often suggest that birthing is hard, dying is difficult and there isn't much ease in between.

Bailey brought some paintings to my new apartment. Certainly I couldn't change history; however, I could trust Bailey to have thought out some of my future.

"Remember what I told you about Malcolm? These same people who didn't appreciate him will revere him in ten years, and you will get in deep trouble if you try to remind them of their earlier attitude.

"Guy is a man-boy. Bright and opinionated. You raised him to think for himself, and now he's doing just that. That's what you asked for, and that's what you've got. When he gets his stuff together, he's going to be a man of principle. Don't worry, he's your son.

"As for you, you'll make a living singing. But that's about all. Nobody knows what you're going to do or who you're going to be. But everybody thinks you're going to do wonderful things. So let's have a drink, and you get busy doing whatever you're s'posed to do."

He was right. I would only eke out a living as a singer. The limited success I had, which Bailey recognized, stemmed from the fact that I didn't love singing. My voice was fair and interesting; my ear was not great, or even good, but my rhythm was reliable. Still, I could never become a great singer, since I would not sacrifice for it. To become wondrously successful and to sustain that success in any profession, one must be willing to relinquish many pleasures and be ready to postpone gratification. I didn't care enough for my own singing to make other people appreciate it.

After six months, the audiences, whose sizes had been respectful, became smaller. A musician told me where my customers had gone.

"There's a real singer down at the Aloha Club, and she's packing them in every night."

On my break I went to the rival club to see my competition. The singer rocked me back in my chair. She was as tall as I, good-looking and very strong. But mainly, she could sing. She had a huge, deep voice, and when she walked on the stage, she owned it. When she nodded to her musicians to start, she reminded me of Joshua and the Battle of Jericho.

> *"Then the lamb, ram, sheep horns began to blow*
> *The trumpets began to sound*
> *Joshua commanded the children to shout*
> *And the walls came tumblin' down."*

The singer stepped up to the microphone unsmiling, wagged her head once to the right and then to the left, the orchestra blared and so did she. Her big dramatic voice windsurfed in that room and walls came tumbling down.

The protective walls I had built around myself as a singer, those that allowed me to sing for convenience, to sing because I could and to sing without rejoicing in the art, all caved in as if obeying the urgency of a load of dynamite.

Listening to Della Reese, I knew I would never call myself a singer again, and that I was going to give up Hawaii and my job at the Encore. I would return to the mainland and search until I found something I loved doing. I might get a job as a waitress and try to finish a stage play I had begun in Accra. I had notebooks full of poems; maybe I'd try to finish them, polish them up, make them presentable and introduce them to a publisher and then pray a lot.

When I thanked Della Reese, I did not mention exactly what she had done for me. I should have said "You've changed my life" or "Your singing made the crooked way straight and the rough road smooth." All I said was "I needed your music, and thank you for giving it so generously." Miss Reese gave me a cool but gracious reply.

The next day I had a meeting with the family in Hawaii and called my mother in San Francisco to tell her that I was moving to Los Angeles. Some former gaping wounds had healed and I was eager. The time had come to return to the mainland, to get a job—to reenter real life.

Uncle Brother gave me the keys to an old Dodge he and Aunt Leah had left in Los Angeles. "It runs when it wants to and goes where it likes, but it ought to serve you till you can do better."

He and Bailey and Aunt Leah, against her better judg-
ment, came down to closing night. My aunt sat primly
throughout the whole show, her arms wrapped around
her body, or she laid her hands in her lap and kept her
gaze upon them.

I had planned to leave Hawaii the next day, so my last
show was not only a farewell to the Encore but to my
family and to the few acquaintances I had made on
Waikiki Beach. As I prepared to go onstage, I thought
about the haven Hawaii had been. I had arrived on the
island in a fragile and unsteady condition. The shock of
Malcolm's murder had demoralized me. There seemed to
be no center in the universe, and the known edges of the
world had become dim and inscrutable.

Leaving Guy in Africa had become a hair shirt that I
could not dislodge. I worried that his newly found and
desperate hold on his mannishness might cause him to
say or do something to irritate the Ghanaian authorities.

I had brought anxiety and guilt to Hawaii, but each
month the worries had abated. Friends in New York
informed me that Malcolm's widow, Betty, had given birth
to healthy twins, and although his dream of an organiza-

tion of African–American unity would not be realized, his family was hale and his friends were true. The actors and writers Ossie Davis and Ruby Dee, attorney Percy Sutton and Alex Haley, who had written Malcolm's biography, were among the steady pillars holding the Shabazz family aloft.

I heard from friends in Ghana that Guy began behaving much better after I left. Often people in general, and young people in particular, need the responsibility of having to depend upon themselves for their own lives.

So I was leaving Hawaii a lighter and brighter person. I was going to Los Angeles, and although I did not know what I would do or whom I would find there, life was waiting on me and it wasn't wise to test its patience.

For that last show on the last night, I decided not to sing but to dance.

I asked for the music, then invited it to enter my body and find the broken and sore places and restore them. That it would blow through my mind and dispel the fogs. I let the music move me around the dance floor.

I danced for the African I had loved and lost in Africa, I danced for bad judgments and good fortune. For moonlight

lying like rich white silk on the sand before the great pyra-
mids in Egypt and for the sound on ceremonial fonton-fron
drums waking the morning air in Takoradi.

The dance was over, and the audience was standing
and applauding. Even Aunt Leah finally looked up and
smiled at me.

Bailey hugged me and gave me a wad of money.

"You're good." He pointed to my heart. "You'll go far."
He said I had what I needed to face another unknown.

I was off to California.

Aloha.

Eight

There is about Los Angeles an air of expectation. Not on the surface, where the atmosphere is lazy, even somnolent, but below the city's sleepy skin, there is a suggestion that something quite delightful might happen and happen soon.

This quiet hope might be the detritus of so many dreams entertained by so many hopefuls as they struggled and pinched and dieted and preened for Hollywood cameras. Possibly those aspirations never really die but linger in the air long after the dreamers have ceased dreaming.

The days in Los Angeles were beautiful. The soft, wavering sunlight gave a filtered golden tint to the streets.

The inhabitants of the working–class neighborhood were obviously house–proud. Little bungalows were cradled confidently on patches of carefully tended lawn, and wind chimes seemed to wait for the breeze on every porch.

I longed for one of those tidy and certain houses. If I could live in a house like that, its absolute rightness of place would spill over and the ragged edges of my life would become neat to match the house.

Frances Williams was the very person I needed. I had known her a decade earlier, and she knew everyone else very well. She was active in Actors' Equity and had connections in both black and white churches.

Fran, as she was called, counseled on the mystery of the theater, on its power and beauty, and gave good advice to anyone smart enough to listen.

She was a large woman with a lusty voice not unlike a cello, and she had a great love of the theater. She and her brother, Bill, lived in a large house at the rear of a corner lot. The house and all the grounds were often pressed into service when Fran directed experimental theater. She had acted in forty movies and had worked as an extra in over a hundred more. When I looked her up, she had exactly what I needed: a place to live and the possibility of a job.

There were two vacant apartments. Each had one room that served as living room, bedroom and study, and each had a large, commodious kitchen. I took one apartment, and Fran told me that the actress Beah Richards took the other.

The apartment was small and dark and humid, so I bought gallons of white latex paint and a stack of rollers and brushes. I painted every inch of visible wall and the entire floor bone-white. I went over the floor with a few coats of adobe enamel. In the lean years before Guy encountered puberty, he and I learned by trial and error how to antique furniture from Salvation Army stores and even how to repair the odd chair or sofa that seemed destined for a junkyard.

I had become such a regular in all Salvation Army and Goodwill stores that salespeople saved certain choice pieces for me. "Maya, how are you? Have I got a fabulous nightstand for you." "Have I got a great dresser for you."

In Los Angeles I bought orange, rust and brown burlap and draped the material casually at windows.

I made huge colorful floor pillows and piled them on the floor. Van Gogh and Matisse posters enlivened the walls.

I stacked painted wood planks on bricks to form bookcases and burned cheap candles in Chianti and Mateus wine bottles. When the melted wax nearly covered the bottles, I put fresh candles in them and placed them around the room for light and esoteric effect.

At little expense, and out of a crying need, I had a house; now I needed a job. The money I brought from Hawaii was sifting through my fingers like fine sand.

Again Fran had the answer. Having lived in Los Angeles since the 1950s, she knew every corner where black people lived. Having worked on their campaigns, she called every elected official by his or her first name.

"This job is called Random Research. You won't be paid much, but you are on an honor system. No one will be going behind you to check on your honesty. You will be given a questionnaire and a district. You will go to every fourth house and ask the housewife the questions on your form."

"What questions?"

"What cereal does your family prefer? What soap powder do you use? What peanut butter do you buy? Like that."

The salary was pitifully low, but the job was blissfully simple. I had started working on my stage play. Random Research would allow me time to develop my characters and plot. I would ask questions of the housewives, but between houses and women and questions and answers, I would let my characters play out plot possibilities. They would find their own voices and design their own personalities.

Watts was my assigned locale, and I was disappointed to find it had lost its air of studied grace. I had known the area when it had a kind of staid decorum, a sort of church-ladies-display-at-a-Sunday-afternoon-tea feeling. The houses were all of the proper size, none so large as to cause envy, none so small as to elicit pity.

Years earlier, the lawns were immaculate, grass was trimmed to an evenness and flowers were carefully placed and lovingly tended. There had not been many people on the street. A drive through residential Watts was like driving through a small town in a 1940s Hollywood movie.

There were always the odd teenagers pumping themselves up on Schwinns, but they could have been extras
in the film, save that these bikers were black, as were
the women who called them home for supper: "Henry,
Henry . . ."

The Watts I visited in 1965 was very different. The
houses were still uniform and similarly painted, and the
lawns still precise, but there were people everywhere.

On my visit to Watts to orient myself for the new job,
I passed groups of men in T-shirts or undershirts, loung-
ing on front porches and steps. Their talk was just a little
louder than usual, and they didn't stop their conversation
or lower their voices when I came into view.

Although I was never pretty, my youth, a good figure
and well-chosen clothes would usually earn a clearing of
the throat, or at least a veiled sound of approval. But the
men in this Watts didn't respond to my presence.

"Good morning, I am working for a company that
wants to improve the quality of the goods you buy. I'd
like to ask you a few questions. Your answers will ensure
that you will find better foods in your supermarket and
probably at a reduced price."

The person who wrote those lines, for interviewers to use with black women, knew nothing of black women. If I had dared utter such claptrap, at best I would have been laughed off the porch or at worst told to get the hell away from the woman's door.

Black females, for the most part, know by the time they are ten years old that the world is not much concerned with the quality of their lives or even their lives at all. When politicians and salespeople start being kind to black women, seeking them out, offering them largesse, the women accept the soft voices, the simpering statements, the often idle promises, because those are likely to be the only flattering behavior directed to them that day. Behind the women's eyes, however, there is a wisdom that does not pretend to be unaware; nor does it permit gullibility.

Martin Luther King, Jr., once related a story that demonstrated just how accurate the black woman was at assessing her location in the scheme of things and knowing how to handle herself wherever she was.

He told us about an older black woman who had worked for a white woman in Alabama, first as her laundress, then as her maid, then as her cook and finally as her housekeeper. After forty years, the black woman retired, but she would go to visit her former employer occasionally.

On one visit, her employer had friends over for lunch. When the employer was told that Lillian Taylor was in the kitchen, she sent for her. Lillian went into the living room and greeted all the women, some of whom she had known since their childhoods.

The white woman said, "Lillian, I know you've heard of the bus boycott."

"Yes, ma'am, I've heard of it."

"Well, I want to know, what do you think of it? Are you supporting it?"

"No, ma'am. Not one bit. Not one little iota. And I won't let none of mine support it, either."

"I knew you'd be sensible, Lillian, I just knew it in my bones."

"Yes, ma'am, I won't touch that bus boycott. You know my son took me to live with him and his family (he won't let me even lift a finger), and he works for the power company way 'cross town from our house. I told him,

'Charles, don't you have anything to do with that bus boycott. You walk to work. Stay all the way out of that bus boycott.' And my grandchildren, they go to school way over on the east side, I told them the same thing: 'Don't have anything to do with that boycott. You walk to school.' And even today, when I wanted to come over and visit you, I got a lady from my church to bring me. I wasn't going to touch that boycott. Sure wasn't."

The room had become quiet, and Lillian Taylor said, "I know you have plenty of help now, but do you want me to bring you all more coffee?"

She went to the kitchen and was followed by the white woman's daughter.

"Lillian, why do you treat my mother like that? Why not just come out and say you support the boycott?"

Lillian said, "Honey, when you have your head in a lion's mouth, you don't snatch it out. You reach up and tickle him behind his ears and you draw your head out gradually. Every black woman in this country has her head in a lion's mouth."

I knew that a straight back and straight talk would get the black woman's attention every time.

"Good morning. I have a job asking questions."

At first there would be wariness. "What questions? Why me?"

"There are some companies that want to know which products are popular in the black community and which are not."

"Why do they care?"

"They care because if you don't like what they are selling, you won't buy, and they want to fix it so you will."

"Yeah, that makes sense. Come on in."

I was never turned away, although most times the women were abstracted. Few gave me their total attention. Some complained that their husbands were around all day.

"I work nights, and usually I come home and sleep a few hours, then get up and have time to fix up my house. But with him not working, he's home all day, bringing his friends in and all that."

Or they complained that the men weren't around.

"I don't know where he's spending his time. He's not working, he's not at the job and he's not at home... makes me a little suspicious."

Listening to the women brought me more squarely back to the U.S.A. The lilt of the language was so beautiful, and I was heartened that being away from the melody for a few years had not made one note foreign to me.

The women ranged from college graduates to those who would find it challenging to read the daily newspaper, yet the burdens of their conversations were the same.

Those who worked or needed medical attention or collected supplemental food stamps were dependent on private cars. Public transportation was so poor that if a woman had to use it in order to be at work by eight-thirty A.M., she would have to leave home at five A.M.

Those who worked as housekeepers, maids and cooks shopped on their way home from their jobs in the stores used by their employers. The goods were fresher, of better quality and remarkably cheaper.

I had gone to Watts to fulfill the demands of my job and had gotten so much more. The women opened their doors and minds to me. Even as I asked about dishwashing Dove and Bold and Crisco and Morton salt, I found hardworking women and hard-thinking women. Indirectly, I met their men, whose jobs had disappeared and who found they were unable to be breadwinners in their own homes.

Some men, embarrassed at their powerlessness, became belligerent, and their wives' bodies showed the extent of their anger. Some, feeling futile, useless, left home, left the places where they read disappointment in every face and heard shame in every voice. Some drank alcohol until they reached the stage of stupor where they could not see or hear and certainly not think.

On the surface, Watts still appeared a pretty American dream, wide thoroughfares, neat lawns, nice bungalows. Those factors were facts, but there is always a truth deeper than what is visible.

Without work and steady salaries, the people could not envision tomorrows. Women and men, furious with themselves and each other, began to abandon the children. They didn't leave them in baskets on doorsteps, they abandoned them in the home. Dinners together became fewer because the father was seldom there and the mother was busy reviewing where she went wrong, or prettying up to set out her lures again.

The bootless children, with discipline removed, without the steadying hand of a present parent who cared, began to run like young tigers in the streets. First their need drove them to others like themselves, with whom they could make a family. Then their rage made the newly formed families dangerous. Gangs of abandoned children bullied their way up and down the sidewalks of Watts, growing bolder and angrier every day.

They left the schools in record numbers. What could school offer them that could be of use? Education, so they could get jobs? But their parents had had jobs that were taken away. Their parents had believed in the system, and see them now? Empty uncaring husks of the people they once were. No. School promised nothing, nothing save a chance to lose the families they had just made and needed so desperately.

Nine

The uproar in Watts taught me something I had not known. Odor travels faster and farther than sound. We smelled the conflagration before we heard it, or even heard about it. The odor that drifted like a shadow over my neighborhood was complex because it was layered. Burning wood was the first odor that reached my nose, but it was soon followed by the smell of scorched food, then the stench of smoldering rubber. We had one hour of wondering what was burning before the television news reporters arrived breathlessly.

There had been no cameras to catch the ignition of the fire. A number of buildings were burning wildly before anyone could film them. Newscasters began to relay the pictures and sounds of the tumult.

"There is full-blown riot in Watts. Watts is an area in southeast Los Angeles. Its residents are predominately Negroes." Pictures were interspersed with the gasps of the newscasters.

That description was for the millions of whites who lived in Los Angeles but who had no idea that Watts existed and certainly no awareness that it was a parcel of the city and only a short ride from their own communities.

Policemen and politicians, all white, came on the television screens to calm down the citizenry in the unscathed regions.

"You have nothing to fear. The police have been deployed to Watts, and in a few hours we will have everything under control."

Those of us who watched the action live on television over the next few days knew that the officials were talking out of their hats.

The rioters had abandoned all concern for themselves, for their safety and freedom. Some threw rocks, stones, cans of beer and soda at police in cars and police on foot.

Heavily burdened people staggered out the doors of super-markets, followed by billows of smoke. Men and women carried electrical appliances in their arms, and some pushed washers and dryers down the middle of the street.

However, nothing—not the voices trained to relay excitement nor the images of unidentifiable looters entering and leaving unlighted shops—could capture the terrifying threat of a riot like the stench of scorched wood and burning rubber.

Radios blared, "Watts is on fire." Television cameras filmed a group of men turning over a car and a young woman throwing a bottle at a superstore window. The glass seemed to break in slow motion. In fact, throughout the duration of the explosion, every incident shown on television seemed acted out at a pace slower than real time.

Sirens screamed through the night, and television screens showed gangs of young men refusing to allow fire trucks a chance to put out fires.

"Burn, baby, burn." The instruction came clear over the radios: "Burn, baby, burn." Certain political analysts observed that the people were burning their own neighborhood. Though few houses were set afire, the rioters considered the stores, including supermarkets, property of the colonialists who had come into the neighborhood to exploit them and take their hard-earned money.

Two days passed and I could wait no longer. I drove to Watts and parked as near the center of the uprising as possible, then I walked. The smell had turned putrid as plastic furniture and supermarket meat departments smoldered. When I reached a main street, I stopped and watched as people pushed piled-high store carts out of burning buildings. Police seemed to be everywhere and nowhere, watching from inside their cars.

A young boy, his arms laden, his face knotted in concentration, suddenly saw me.

"You want a radio?"

I was amazed that there was no guilt in his voice. I said, "No, not yet. Thanks anyway."

Ordinarily I would have read in the boy's face, or felt, an "Uh-huh, this woman knows I've been stealing." There would have been at least an ounce of shame. But his approach had been conspiratorial, as if to say, "We're in this together. I know you not only know what I am doing, you approve of it and would do it yourself if you could."

Smoke and screams carried in the air. Someone behind me was cursing long, keen streaks of profanity. It became hard to discern if the figures brushing past me were male or female, young or old.

The farther I walked, the more difficult it was to breathe. I had turned and started back to my car when a sound cut the air. The loud whine of police sirens was so close it stabbed into my ears. Policemen in gas masks emerged out of the smoke, figures from a nightmare. Alarm flooded me, and in a second I was dislocated. It seemed that the sirens were in my nose, and smoke packed my ears like cotton. Two policemen grabbed a person in front of me. They dragged the man away as he screamed, "Take your hands off me, you bastards! Let me go!"

I ran, but I couldn't see the pavement, so it was nearly impossible to keep my footing. I ran anyway. Someone grabbed for me, but I shrugged off the hand and continued running. My lungs were going to burst, and my calves were cramping. I pushed myself along. I was still running when I realized I was breathing clean air. I read the street signs and saw that I was almost a mile away from my car, but at least I wasn't in jail. Because I had run in the opposite direction from where I had parked, I would have to circle Watts to find my car, but at least I wasn't in Watts.

When I returned home, the television coverage was mesmerizing. The National Guard was shown arriving in Watts. They were young men who showed daring on their faces but fear in their hearts. They were uncomfortable with new, heavy responsibilities and new, heavy guns.

After three days the jails began to fill. The media covered hundreds of looters being arrested. Frances Williams said that the rumor in the neighborhood beauty salons and barbershops was that the police were arresting anyone black and those suspected of being black.

Watts was all anyone could think of. The fact of it, the explosion of anger, surprised and befuddled some: "I've driven through Watts many times. It's very nice." Some people were furious: "The police should have the right to shoot at will. If a few of those looters were shot, the rest would get the message soon enough." Watts went on burning. It had not had enough, and I hadn't had enough.

Curiosity had often lured me to the edge of ruin. For years, I had known that there is nothing idle about curiosity, despite the fact that the two words are often used in tandem. Curiosity fidgets, is hard to satisfy, looks for answers even before forming questions. Curiosity wants to behold, to comprehend, maybe even to become.

Two days after my tentative foray into the war zone, I had to go again, but this time I wouldn't allow fear any control over me. This time I would not run.

The combustion had spread, so my previous parking space was now only a block from the riot. I parked there anyway and walked directly into the din.

Burglar alarms continued to ring in the stores that had no front doors or windows. Armed civilians stood in front of ravaged businesses, guarding against further looting. They were heckled.

"Hey, brother, you guarding Charlie's thing. You must be a fool."

"I sure wouldn't risk my life for somebody else's stuff. If they care that much for it, they ought to come down here and look after it themselves."

"Ain't that much money in the world make me lose my life . . ."

The National Guard was heckled, too, but not as pointedly.

"Hey, man, you drew some lame duty."

"Don't you feel like a fool standing in front of a super-market?"

I heard this in front of a pawnshop: "Hey, man, don't you feel stupid keeping people from stealing something that was already stole in the first place?"

The soldiers worked at keeping straight faces.

The devastation was so much broader. On the second day of the riot, and my first day visiting Watts, there was a corridor of burned-out buildings and cars, but on the fourth day, the corridor had widened substantially.

That night I sat down at my kitchen table and wrote on a yellow pad my description of the events I had seen in Watts and the uprising as it was reported on television.

Our

YOUR FRIEND CHARLIE *pawnshop*

was a glorious blaze

I heard the flames lick

then eat the trays

of zircons

mounted in red-gold alloys

Easter clothes and stolen furs

burned in the attic
radios and TVs
crackled with static
plugged in
only to a racial outlet

Hospitality, southern-style
cornpone grits and you-all smile
whole blocks novae
brand-new stars
policemen caught in their
brand-new cars
Chugga chugga chigga
git me one nigga
lootin' n burnin'
he won't git far

Lighting: a hundred Watts
Detroit, Newark and New York
Screeching nerves, exploding minds
lives tied to
a policeman's whistle
a welfare worker's doorbell
finger

Spirit walked with me on my second visit to the exploding section of Watts. I became invisible in the black community. I had to stop and stand still when I realized that no one seemed to see me. When I had visited Watts on the first day of my new job, no one spoke to me or commented on my presence, but I was seen. This time I could have been in a white neighborhood. When a black person appears in a white part of town, there is a moment of alarm, but if the black doesn't appear threatening, he is erased from the white mind immediately.

In the black community, a black person is always given her humanity.

On this visit to Watts, the responses were different. Neither the looters, the police, the spectators nor the National Guard took notice of me. A group of young men was bouncing a car filled with white passengers whose faces looked like Halloween masks through the car windows. Terror bulged from their eyes, and if the windows had been open, I would have heard the screams pouring out of their wide, gaping mouths.

A phalanx of police slipped by me and were upon the rioters quickly and quietly. The officers began handcuffing the offenders, and I turned my attention to the now settled car. Its inhabitants were exchanging smiles that I didn't read as smiles of relief, but rather of satisfaction. They had come to Watts to get a thrill, and hadn't they done just that?

The newly arrested men were marched close enough for me to touch them, but neither they nor the police regarded me.

I came upon some people who were sauntering down the main street, casually taking in the sights. They were so at ease in that uneasy time and place that it was obvious they lived in the neighborhood. Their concentration was on the stores and the burned-out shells of buildings, so they didn't see me.

The havoc now had areas of calm, and either I brought serenity with me or it found me wherever I was. I watched as people sifted through debris. Each whole cup or unbroken plate was treated as a treasure. A woman smiled with pleasure when she found a matched pair of shoes. A man passed me carrying a pair of well-worn pants and grinning.

On the first day of insurgency, people of all ages allowed their rage to drive them to the streets. But on the fourth day, the anger of the older citizens was spent. I read sadness and even futility on their faces. But I saw no one attempt to dissuade the younger rioters from their hurly-burly behavior.

People in front of and behind me were taken to jail, and I was ignored. Admittedly, I didn't curse or shout at the law enforcers, nor did I carry anything that even faintly resembled loot, but that had not influenced the police earlier. People on their way to or from work had been apprehended.

The night before, I had remembered one of my mother's statements: "Nothing's wrong with going to jail for something you believe in. Remember, jail was made for people. Not horses." That is when I had decided I would return to Watts ready to be arrested.

Three police vans were filled and driven away as I stood on the corner of 125th and Vermont. I headed back to my car with an equal mixture of disappointment and relief.

The upheaval continued in volume and drama for five days, and although the violence waned, the frustration was as pervasive as ever. Politicians and community representatives met and held press conferences. Viewers were told that a plan for Watts was being hammered out.

The ash had not yet settled on every car and windowsill before the streets were filled with tourists who came to look at Watts. Journalists from France, England and the Soviet Union were shown on television interviewing people in Watts. They asked any question that came to mind: "Why did Watts burn?" "Why did you burn your own neighborhood?" "Isn't America supposed to be the melting pot?" "Were you trying to get the heat up to melting temperature?"

The people answered with anything that came to their minds.

"It burned down before I noticed."

"I didn't have a job, so I burned down Watts."

"I didn't have anything else to do, so I burned a store."

The journalists were being treated with the old-as-slavery response: "If a white man asks where you're going, you tell him where you've been."

A white man asks, "Where are you going, boy?" Your response should be, with much head scratching and some shuffling, "You know, boss, I was down that street over there by that big old tree, you know, and I saw something 'twas hard to look upon . . ."

"I didn't ask where you were, I asked where are you going."

"Yes sir, that's what I'm trying to tell you. If you had seen what I've seen . . . I don't . . . if they're . . . couldn't have been a half a mile away. I had to get out of there, or I don't know what would have happened."

The white man would usually respond, "Oh, you're a fool. I'm not going to waste any more time on you." The white man walks away, and the black man is pleased that no secrets were revealed or any lies told.

But talking drums of the black community carried the message loud and clear. The rebellion reached some important ears, and things were going to change. Community spokespersons said what was needed most was a medical clinic so that sick people didn't have to travel two or three hours just to see a doctor.

The unemployed wanted jobs, the underemployed wanted better jobs.

Who would answer all the questions, fulfill all the requests? Would anyone? Could anyone? History had taught the citizens of Watts to hope for the best and expect nothing, but be prepared for the worst.

A shaft of sunlight penetrated the gloom of cynicism when Budd Schulberg, an award-winning writer, went to Watts and founded the Watts Writers Workshop. People who didn't know his name would bless him forevermore.

"He's a Hollywood writer, you say?"

"And he's coming to Watts?"

"Here's one white man who's putting his body where his mouth is. I like that. I sure do."

Some women, mostly white, largely the wives of film moguls, banded together to form an organization, Neighbors of Watts. They went to the area to ask the women how they could be of help.

Mrs. Violetta Robinson, often called the Mother of Watts, told them what the women of Watts needed—an accredited, well-funded child-care center so that they could leave their children and go to work with clear minds. Something of slavery lurked in the shadows of that request. Slave mothers, up before sunrise and sleeping after dark, went to the canebrakes and cotton fields with minds less clouded with concern because they knew a woman, Aunt Susie, Aunty Mae, Aunt Carrie, would be looking after all the children. They took satisfaction in the fact that "Aunt Susie loves children." The children "just love Aunty Mae." "Aunt Carrie won't stand for no foolishness from the children, but she would feed them herself. She won't let them eat from a trough like hogs as some did on other plantations." Sometimes the children's plates were corn husks or cabbage leaves; still, each child ate with clean fingers and from a clean surface.

One hundred and fifty years later, black women still needed that same assurance.

My landlady, who knew everything, said the Neighbors of Watts were going to provide a child-care center. She also said a medical institute was going to be built in Watts, and that it would be named for Charles Drew, a great African-American doctor who developed a technique to separate out plasma from whole blood.

A French journalist telephoned me and said James Baldwin had given him my name and number. I agreed to an interview. He sat, contained, on my studio bed-cum-sofa.

"We French, we have never, never, never had slavery, so we feel we don't understand the American racism."

Maybe it was that third "never" that made me pick him up and dust him off.

"What did you call Haiti? A resort?"

Suddenly his English failed him. "Haiti? *Est-ce que tu a dit Haiti?*"

I said, "*Oui.*"

He said, "I meant in France. *Nous* have *jamais* had *esclavage* on the land of France."

I said, "You were the rulers of Haiti and Martinique — and Guadeloupe. None of the Africans went there on the *Ile de France.* They were taken there on slave ships."

He said he was beginning to understand the rage a little. If people like me were so angry, how much angrier were those who had less than I?

I looked at the man, his beret, his neat little dancing hands, and looked at my studio apartment with its furniture from Goodwill and its prints from Woolworth's. I had less than many others I knew, but if he thought I was well-off, then nothing I could say would help him understand Watts. If he had visited the area one day before it exploded, if he had gone to the right bar or pool hall or community center, he could have met someone who heard his accent and, realizing he was a stranger, might have invited him home.

He could have been sitting in a well-furnished house dining on great chicken and greens, receiving all the kindnesses. Then he really would have been befuddled if, on the following day, he heard of the conflagration and had seen his host of the day before struggling with the heavily armed police.

But I could not needle him. He was not going to comprehend the anger and disappointment in Watts, and further provoking him was not going to make me feel better. Like many of my ancestors, I settled back to tell him some of what he wanted to hear and some of what I wanted to say.

Surely he returned to Paris with some truth and some fiction. Surely he wrote an account of the Watts riot allowing his readers to hold on to the stereotypes that made them comfortable while congratulating themselves on being in possession of some news.

Ten

Frank Silvera was exactly what is meant in South America by the word *mestizo*. His ancestors were African and Spanish, and he was a light-skinned black man who could play a Mexican father to Marlon Brando's Zapata. A black man who could play an Italian father to Ben Gazzara in *A Hatful of Rain* on Broadway. A black man who could play the title role of Shakespeare's *King Lear*.

Silvera had a theater company in Los Angeles that he named the Theatre of Being or, as the member actors called it, Tee Oh Bee. Beah Richards, my next-door neighbor, was the star of the company, with Vantile Whitfield and Dick Anthony Jones as resident leading men.

Beah, with her success on and off Broadway and particularly in James Baldwin's *The Amen Corner*, was a legend in the African-American community. At the time I met her, she was often called our greatest stage actress, vying only with Ruby Dee for that honor.

Frank decided to stage *Medea* at his Theatre of Being. Naturally, Beah would take the title role. And just as naturally, she would take it beyond all real or imagined limits. When Frank announced the project, Beah and I and a few friends celebrated. In the middle of that evening's festivities, problems were mentioned. Beah didn't drive. I offered to take her to the theater each day, and she said she would pay for the gas.

The role of the nurse had not been filled. I joined the line of actors auditioning, and, using a Langston Hughes poem and a Shakespearean sonnet, I was given the role of the nurse.

I knew I was adequate, but I was never sure if Frank hired me because of my talent or to ensure that Beah had a way to get to the theater.

Frank and Beah shared a profound mutual admiration. She would speak, and he would either laugh uproariously or stroke his chin and pace the floor, lost in a deep brown study.

Rehearsals further increased my insecurity. I would stand backstage as Frank consistently positioned Beah center stage under the bright beams. Of course she was the star, but the role of the nurse was not irrelevant, and he never called on me. I began to smart in the shadows. I went to a bookstore and bought Euripides' version of *Medea*, as well as every book I could find about Medea, Jason, the *Argo* and the Golden Fleece.

There was a neighborhood bar next to the theater. I informed the stage manager that I could be found in the bar whenever I was wanted. Each day I would drop Beah off, greet folks in the theater, then go to sit at a table in the dimly lit bar. I worked out who the nurse was and why she was so loyal to Medea.

In my created version of the play's history, Nurse had been the midwife at Medea's birth. Nurse had a baby just after Medea was born, but Nurse's baby died. Medea's mother, not wanting the bother, persuaded Nurse to become a nurse cow and give to Medea the dead child's milk.

In the bar, I built my character, her whims and her whimsy. I decided early on that Nurse thought of Medea as her own daughter and doted on the girl. As Medea grew into womanhood, Nurse cherished her, idolized her and followed her everywhere, walking as precisely as possible in her footsteps. When Medea married Jason, Nurse attended the ceremony. When Medea stole the fleece of pure gold from her father, the king, because Jason asked her to do so, Nurse helped her. Nurse later escaped the king's rage by joining Medea on the Argonauts' ship, the *Argo*. Nurse was crippled by arthritis because she often slept on the ground. She didn't mind the discomfort as long as she was near Medea. She had grown old and dotty in service to Medea, who took Nurse's worship as her due. Maddened by rage at Jason's growing coldness toward her, Medea killed their two sons. Nurse knew of the murders but gave Medea no rebuke, saying, "She did what any woman would have done if provoked."

I began taking license with the simply told story of passion and horror. Since I was not directed, I had to create situations that would explain why the character I was playing could condone even the most base actions of Medea. I did not propose to comprehend Medea's mind, or how love and idolatry could lead to theft and murder, but I did find that Nurse had a fair voice, and singing was the only pleasure she had that didn't stem from Medea.

I got some stage gray hair and ghoulish makeup, and a week before opening, when I was invited to join rehearsal, I brought the gray-haired, limping, singing nurse onto the stage. Beah and Frank were amazed, and neither was too pleased, but we were too close to opening for Frank to redirect me.

The play opened to baffling reviews. Some critics loved it, while others loathed it. Some thought it modern and wonderfully acted, and some thought it stagey and mannered. All lauded Beah Richards, and a few had kind words for the elderly actress whom no one knew but who played the nurse so well.

Eleven

Sid's Café and Bar was a popular hangout for people from New Orleans. The owner, Jase, and his wife, Marguerite, were highly respected cooks of Louisiana food, and the bar was always filled with bright laughter and loud talk. Jase and Marguerite liked and welcomed me, so Sid's became my base.

One evening a group of four in the red booth at the front of the café were particularly interesting. The two women were as loud and fierce as the men, yet no one used profanity. They saw me watching, and one man beckoned me over.

"Hey, are you alone?"

I said, "Yes."

"Well, join us."

"Yes, come on." I sat. "Are you from New Orleans?"

"No."

"Well, we are. Where did you run away from?"

"I came here from Hawaii, and before that, San Francisco, and before that, Ghana in West Africa."

"Hey, all right. You will fit right in with me. I am one crazy lying nigger, too. My name is Phil. What's yours?"

"My name is Maya, and I am neither a nigger nor a liar."

One woman said, "That's right. Speak up for yourself. This fool calls himself a nigger, and he'd put his fist through the face of the first white man using that word."

"I can say it 'cause I am me. I don't mean any harm."

I said, "But you're calling yourself a despicable word, and surely you are not despicable."

Phil said, "I believe you were in Hawaii and Africa. You sound a little like a teacher I had in Baton Rouge."

I said, "I thought you were from New Orleans."

Phil said, "Told you I was a lying nigger. I can be ornery, too."

I said, "Maybe I'd better go back to my table."

Everyone spoke at once.

"No. Stay with us."

"Tell us about Africa."

"No, I want to hear about Hawaii."

"Don't mind Phil. He really doesn't mean any harm, and we do laugh a lot."

I enjoyed the group's company, and after I had been around them a few weeks, Phil used the racial slur less. When he did slip, he would pop out his eyes and look straight at me.

One morning they came to my house. I offered them Mogen David and Mateus wine. We sat around the kitchen table drinking and telling stories.

Phil suggested that we go for a ride. We agreed, although we were all too old to be joyriding, since the youngest of us had to be at least thirty.

There were no dissenters. We all piled into Phil's run-down car and said things like:

"Home, James, and don't spare the horses."

"Driver, follow that cab."

"There's a tenner in it for you if you keep him in sight."

We were in high spirits as we crossed railroad tracks and heard a train whistle blow. We began to imitate the sound. After a second, Phil backed up until our car sat on the tracks. He turned off the motor.

I couldn't see the train, but judging by the sound of the whistle, it was just around a curve in the tracks.

I shouted, "Move the car. Move the damn car." I was sitting in the backseat. Phil turned his head to look at me and grinned.

I pushed on the back of the front passenger seat, but the woman in it had gone to sleep. Another voice joined mine as the train rounded into view. "Move, man, what the hell?" I had begun to scream. "You are going to get us killed."

The motor turned over, and the car slid off the tracks seconds before the train sped behind us.

The two passengers in the backseat with me cursed Phil roundly, but I couldn't speak. I had been frightened mute again, just like twenty-five years earlier, when I had been so terrorized that I had chosen to become mute.

This time I had no choice. Words simply would not come. Phil stopped the car on the corner by my house.

"You want to get out here?"

I nodded.

The woman sitting next to him awakened grouchy. "What's going on?" She frowned and leaned forward. I crawled out around her. When I was standing beside the car, I realized that I had urinated. My clothes were wet and crumpled.

When Phil waited for me to walk away, I decided he must have known I had been scared enough to pee on myself. I could not stand there all day, so I crossed the street in front of the car to give him a good chance to see me.

His laughter did not surprise me. "I scared the piss out of her. Look. Yes, I did . . . Maya, come back and clean up my car. Come back, I won't do it again."

I continued walking to my house. He drove slowly beside me, laughing, urging me to get back in the car. His taunting did not embarrass me. The level of my fear totally outweighed everything he said.

He didn't drive off until I walked up the steps to my house.

As I showered, the terror released me. In clean, dry clothes, I sat down and thought about the horrible incident.

I remembered Phil's self-description when I first met him, and I realized that I had learned at least one important lesson. Believe people when they tell you who they are. They know themselves better than you. The racial pejorative might not have applied to him. I didn't know him well enough to know if he was or wasn't a liar, but I found out he was certainly mean and he was ornery.

Twelve

The telephone voice startled me.

"Hello, is this my Maya?"

Shock closed my throat.

"Hello, Maya, speak to me. This is your husband."

He wasn't my husband, but he was my great love and my greatest fear, and I had left him in Africa. "Hello," I answered, reluctantly.

"I am here." He couldn't be. I looked at the door. "I am in New York City. I have come to the States to collect you. God gave you to me. Remember?"

I couldn't speak.

He was the man I felt had taken the heart out of my

body and worn it boldly on his shoulder like an epaulette, and I had adored him.

He said, "Do you still love me?"

I finally asked, "Are you really in New York City?"

He continued, as was his way. "Of course you love me. I am coming to California to collect you and take you back to Africa."

I told him that I had made a life for myself in Los Angeles and I was not going anywhere.

We had both worked on trying to establish a relationship in Ghana. He was loud, bombastic and autocratic. But he loved me and found me funny and sexy, and he said I was brilliant. He was astonishingly handsome, and his upbringing as a young royal gave him an assurance that I had found irresistible. We might have succeeded at being together, but I had no precedent for being who he wanted me to be. I did love him, but that had not been enough. He needed to be worshiped. Being an American, a black American woman, being Vivian Baxter's daughter, Bailey Johnson's sister and Guy Johnson's mother, I was totally unprepared to worship any mortal.

We had argued loudly and reconciled feverishly so

many times that I knew our lives would always follow that pattern. I had come to that realization at the same time that my son had found "mother" to be a useless word, so I was often addressed as "Yeah."

I had left Africa to him and to my African love. And now my lover was on the same continent, and I had no place to run.

I called my mother for her strength and guidance. Her voice was warm and loving.

"Baby, it's a big world, and Los Angeles is a big city. He can come. Los Angeles can hold both of you."

She hadn't heard him roaring at me, or me screaming back at him.

"Oh yes," she went on, "I spoke to Guy the other day. He's about finished at school, and I think I hear home-coming in his talk."

"Oh?"

"Yes, he'll want to come home when he finishes. But he's out of money."

"Mom, I left him enough to live on, so if he's squan-dered—"

She said, "He's my grandson. I won't see him needy."

"That's between you and your grandson, but when he is ready to come home, I'll give you the money for his fare. Just don't let him know."

Mother said, "I understand," and she did.

The African arrived and filled my little studio apartment with his loud voice and his maleness. His sexuality was so evident that I thought everyone could perceive it.

He charmed my landlady and my neighbor. When he told them that he had come to take me back to Africa, they both offered to help me pack.

My body was in a state of utter bliss, but I could not mask my displeasure that he wanted to be waited upon as if he were an invalid: "Get this." "Fetch that." "Make food for me."

I knew English was not his first language; still, I had to tell him that "fetch" was an old-fashioned word used during slavery and I would not respond favorably to it.

On some evenings I wondered what I would do without him. On some evenings we talked about my concerns and he listened. On some evenings he held me and let me cry about Malcolm.

I would moan and say, "Black men shot him, what's the matter with us?"

"You are human. That is a historic problem. Remember, Cain killed Abel. His brother."

"But what will our people do? It took a long time to make Malcolm."

"You've got a long time. Some say that the American Negro represents the best the African can hope for."

He looked at my surprise.

"I agree in part. Sold by your people, brought here as slaves. Slavery lasted nearly three hundred years, and ten, twenty years after it was abolished, you had schools. Colleges. Fisk, Howard, Tuskegee. And even today, look at you, you are everywhere in this country. You will be all right." He patted me and hugged me.

When he was good, he was very very good. Ah. But when he was bad . . .

I went to my friend the actress Nichelle Nichols. We had become friends ten years earlier, during the filming of *Porgy and Bess.*

She was beautiful even when scowling. "Girl, tell him he is in America now, and we believe in one person, one vote. Anyway, bring him over for dinner. I'll have a little bee for his bonnet."

After fifteen minutes, I saw that dinner at Nichelle's was a bad idea. He spoke of Mother Africa and her children everywhere, and Nichelle was spellbound.

As we left, she whispered to me, "You're so lucky."

Thirteen

Los Angeles, seen through my lover's eyes, was more colorful than I had realized, more variegated. He saw Watts as a community of great interest. After he observed many black families trying to restore their neat neighborhoods, he said, "But these people are fastidious."

I was surprised at his surprise. He explained, "Until recently in Africa all we saw of American Negroes was Rochester with Jack Benny, and Stepnfetchit, and athletes like Joe Louis and Jackie Robinson. I haven't seen it, but I understand Harlem is a hellhole."

"Harlem is beautiful."

In every conversation with him, I put on my armor of

defense, whether I needed it or not, and whether or not my point of view was defensible.

"There are a few ugly places," I admitted, "but there are many ugly places in Africa."

We visited black-owned bookstores that featured books by blacks and about blacks.

He bought out entire shelves' worth and asked me to pay. The money was his, but he asked me to carry it, saying that he could not understand paper money without a black man's face on it.

I sidestepped a full-out argument by not reminding him that the Ghanaian pound, with Kwame Nkrumah's face on it, was only ten years old.

I was in a labyrinth, going somewhere without knowing my destination or even when I might arrive. I still loved him and wanted him, but there were parts of his life I could not even begin to fathom.

Sometimes, when I answered my telephone, a woman's voice would ask for him. She was calling from New York.

My lover explained, "She is a very old black lady, and she was helpful to me when I stopped at the United Nations."

Her voice didn't sound old, and he laughed with her on the telephone as if she were a girl.

"Her name is Dolly McPherson, and she is a very powerful old woman. She is an official at the Institute of International Education."

Our final argument came unexpectedly over Doris Day and Rock Hudson. We had gone to a movie in which they starred. He was totally silent as I drove home. He didn't speak when we got out of the car or when we entered the house. He was pouting. I didn't know why, and I was certainly not going to ask. I hated the torture of the silent treatment that he used when he was displeased.

I went straight to the kitchen and began warming the food I had cooked earlier. When the table was set with my good china and dinner placed on my best tablecloth, I went into the living room, where he sat like a Yoruba carving.

"Dinner is ready."

He looked up at me, his eyes glinting and his face in a monumental scowl.

"Why can't we be like them?"

"Like whom?"

"Those two actors in the film."

"Doris Day and Rock Hudson?"

"I don't know their names, but why can't we be to each other the way they are?"

"Are you serious?"

"Do you think I am playing?"

"Those are actors. They are not real. I mean, the roles are just roles. You know that."

He had graduated from England's top university with the highest academic degree and he was one of the most educated persons I had ever known. He was being perverse.

Perversity is contagious. I asked, "You want me to become a perky little blond woman? Is that what you want? You have little chance of getting that from me."

He said, "You American Negroes. I never know if you are just stupid or merely pretending." He looked at me pityingly.

Cursing has never been one of my strong suits, but I gathered a few sordid words and started throwing them around. The louder I became, the more scornful his look, and the louder I became.

I picked up my car keys and my purse and went into the kitchen. I took the corners of the tablecloth and let the food and plates and silverware and glasses fall down in the center. I dragged the whole thing to the living room.

"Here's dinner if you want it. I'm leaving."

Anger and frustration rode with me all the way to Nichelle's house.

"Well, Maya, you're always welcome to stay here, but you know how I feel about your marriage."

We weren't married. In Ghana we had done a little homemade ritual in the presence of a few friends. There had been no public ceremony, no authority to sanction our being together, no license assuring us of society's agreement. We had said some words, made some promises and poured schnapps on the ground.

I called my mother in San Francisco, who said that Bailey was visiting. I spoke to my brother and told him of my predicament. He listened and said that they would both be in Los Angeles the next day. I told them that I was spending the night with Nichelle and gave them the phone number and address.

They arrived at Nichelle's house in the morning in a rental car and I filled them in over coffee. I mentioned the African's cold treatment and how it drove me mad. They both understood. I said nothing about the curse words.

Mom said, "Well, let's go over and meet this man who wants to take you back to Africa."

Bailey rode in my car. He had been my closest and dearest friend all my life. "My, how is it? What do you want?"

"I want him to go back to Africa. He brings no peace, and I can't seem to manufacture any while he is around. He should go."

Bailey said, "Then he will go, and go today. Somewhere."

My brother was black and beauteous. He had given me my name, protected me, educated me and told me when I was twelve that I was smart. He had added that I was not as smart as he was, but I was smarter than almost everyone else. He was, at his tallest, five feet four inches tall.

The African had showered and changed, but the soiled tablecloth remained on the floor.

He shook hands with Bailey and embraced my mother.

Mother looked at the litter on the floor and turned to me.

"I left it here last night."

Mother said, "Aha."

I nodded to Bailey. He helped me carry the sour-smelling bundle back to the kitchen. Mother sat down, and as Bailey and I left the room, I heard her say, "Now, what's going on between you and my baby?"

Bailey asked me, "Where are his clothes? Does he have enough money to leave?" I pointed to a closet and told him that the African had plenty of money. I added, "He said he had brought a lot because he was going to carry me back to Africa."

Bailey said, "The hell. Did he think he had to pay a bride-price?"

That was my brother. He could make me laugh even in the grimmest situations.

"He's been talking about going to Mexico City. Kwesi Brew is Ghana's ambassador to Mexico, and Kwesi and his wife, Molly, love him. They dote on him."

Bailey said, "From what I see, he can take a lot of doting."

He watched as I cleared up the mess. "You are really your mother's daughter. He doesn't know he is lucky that you didn't dump that dinner on his head."

I told him that if I had done that, I thought the African would have hit me.

Bailey responded instantly, "He'd have only one time to do that. Next time he'd draw back a stub. Let's go see what your mother is doing."

My little mother sat in the one upholstered chair as primly as an old-fashioned schoolteacher. Her legs were crossed at the ankles. Her purse and gloves lay in her lap.

"Well, baby, this gentleman has reported you to me. He said you used profanity last night."

The African blurted out, "She used words I never even heard Negro sailors use when their ships docked in Ghana's port city of Tema. Her mouth should be washed out. You should do that."

Mother said, "Oh, I would never do a thing like that. Never. People use profanity because they have limited vocabularies or because they are lazy or too frustrated to search for the words they want. My daughter has an extensive vocabulary and doesn't have a lazy bone in her body. So she cursed out of frustration. Why were you frustrated, baby?"

Bailey spoke before I could answer. "Excuse me, Mom, but I'd like to speak to him." He turned to the African. "Would you come with me for a walk around the block?"

The African assented. When they were both on the steps, Bailey stuck his head back in the door.

"Pack his clothes."

Mother watched as I folded the flamboyant African robes into a trunk.

"Your brother said you didn't sound right on the telephone. That's why we are here."

"I wasn't right. I won't deny I was happy to see him, but I can't stand his rudeness in my face all the time."

"Wasn't he rude in Africa?" Although it was ten A.M., she was making herself a Scotch. She had told me years earlier that the time to drink was when you wanted it and could afford to buy it for yourself.

"It wasn't so bad there. First he had his business to focus his attention. He had his children, and I had my own house. And here he's only got me. So since he can't stand anyone around me, I've become the whipping boy."

Mother sucked her teeth loudly. "Well, you sure as hell weren't raised to be that for anybody. But it's all right. Your brother will take care of it."

The two men walked back into the house laughing uproariously and patting each other on the back.

"I want you to come to Africa yourself, Bailey, see how we live, eh."

Bailey said, "You bet. I'll probably be there before Maya gets back." He noticed my suitcase on the floor. He asked, "Oh, you've been packing?"

I said, "Yes, this is mine. I'm going back up to San Francisco with you and Mom." I wanted to save my lover's face. "I packed for him, too." I pointed to the luggage in the corner. "He's been talking to friends in Mexico City."

The African said, "That's where I'm going, and I'm going today. I will telephone Kwesi Brew. He will meet me."

I offered to make breakfast. Bailey shook his head. "I'm taking him to a great breakfast place in Venice. You need to make reservations for one from Los Angeles to Mexico City." Bailey and Mother went into the kitchen so my lover and I could have privacy. We embraced emotionally.

"You could come with me . . ."

I was already missing him. I said, "Not now, later. But why did you decide so suddenly to go?"

"Your brother. He talked to me, man to man. There seems to be something in my personality that rubs you the wrong way, and I may threaten, or at least weaken, your decision to return to me and Africa. So, at his suggestion, I am leaving you some space. He really loves you. You are lucky. But he understands me, and that's more important. He has retained more of the African spirit than you or your mother."

I could have kicked him. He was doing the very thing that had run me away from him in Africa. He so routinely disparaged other people's importance that he didn't notice he was degrading me.

"You can come to Mexico or I'll come back here. I mean to take you back."

Bailey said he would telephone about the reservation. I wished my love a safe journey and asked to be remembered to Kwesi and Molly Brew.

He was gone.

. . .

Bailey and Mother left that same day, but not before rag-
ging me about the inane predicament I had created for
myself.

"It's time for the troubleshooters to move on. You
must not think you can call out the troops at each rumor
of war."

I didn't call them to come. Or perhaps I did. Despera-
tion may have been in my voice, must have been there,
but I did not ask outright that they come to Los Angeles
to rescue me. I was a woman, not a child. My name was
spelled double-you oh em a en.

No, I didn't ask, but I was extremely glad they had
come.

Fourteen

Despite acres of ravaged city blocks and hulks of burned-out cars, Los Angeles seemed to have settled back into a satisfied-with-itself air. The cauldron still simmered in a few quarters, but the energy was spent and it would not boil over again anytime soon.

I had finished writing my play, and I asked Frank Silvera for advice. "Find a producer and give it to him. It will be his job to find the money, the theater, a director and a cast."

I said to him that he had not had to use those tactics; he had done everything himself.

He reminded me that he was the owner, producer and director of Tee Oh Bee.

I searched diligently for a producer, but there was a dearth of them interested in a new play by an unknown playwright who also happened to be black and female. Few would even read the manuscript. Coming out of the shadow of the Watts revolt, they thought the plot would lean heavily on racial unrest.

My plot in *All Day Long*, admittedly slight, was based on one day in the life of a poor thirteen-year-old black boy who was relocated to the North. Among his many travails were the difficulty of understanding the Northern accent and comprehending how a sofa could secretly contain a bed larger than any he had ever seen.

In my play, the boy worked through his befuddlement at flushing toilets (where did it all go?), the mystery of a refrigerator that stayed cold without a block of ice in it and the gift of fresh water that came through hardened silver tubes. A slim idea, but I remembered my own stupefaction when Bailey and I returned to California as teenagers after ten years in the rural South. In Arkansas we had drawn water from a well, and for baths we had heated it on a wood-burning stove. We slept on mattresses stuffed with feathers from chickens we raised and killed and ate, and used a shack away from the house as a toilet.

So a foldout sofa and an indoor toilet had been miracles of modernity to me. I found no one interested enough to produce *All Day Long.*

Back to the library. I had to learn how to produce. All I discovered there was that producing meant having money, and most of the people I knew had very little; the few who were well-off weren't interested in my play.

Kwame Nkrumah, the president of Ghana, was deposed while on a visit to China. It appeared that the time was out of joint, which meant that even if I wanted to return to Africa, Ghana was out of the question for me. I had been a devout Nkrumaist.

In just two years, Malcolm had been murdered and the Watts conflagration had left a roster of arrestees, hundreds homeless and many hurt. My once great love affair hadn't worked out the second time, and now a person I had supported and admired was in exile from his country. I knew how Africans build their lives around their land, their families and friends. I wept for Kwame Nkrumah, for Ghana, for Africa, and some tears were for me.

Fifteen

I sensed my friend Nichelle pulling away from me. I knew I was tenderhearted and a little paranoid, but I felt that she disapproved of me for sending the African away. I thought that she believed I was too hasty in letting go of the man who seemed to her to have been so desirable for me. He had status, intelligence, money and charisma. I might not do better than that anywhere.

Beah Richards was my neighbor, and we were friendly but never close friends. Professor M. J. Hewitt, a beautiful green-eyed friend with whom I was close, had found a great love and gone off to South America with him.

I noted the signs and determined that the time had come for me to be moving on.

My deliberations were focused on where to go. San Francisco didn't beckon, Hawaii held nothing for me. I began to look at New York.

I telephoned Bailey, who had moved back from Hawaii to San Francisco. "Of course, go to New York. As long as you don't get involved in the politics."

Mother came to the phone and said, "That's all right. But don't forget you can always come home."

A letter from the African's elderly lady friend in New York helped me decide definitely that I should head back East. Dolly McPherson wrote:

Dear Miss Angelou,

I am going into the hospital for surgery. I'll probably take a month to completely recover, but if you want to come to New York, I'll try to help you get settled. Possibly I can help you find employment if you need it.

Our African friend told me so much about you I can hardly wait to get to know you. If you'd like to send me your resume, I'll be glad to look it over and see how I might be of help.

Yours,

Dolly McPherson

The friendliness in the letter made me bless the sweetness of old black women. I began to look forward to meeting her. I was sure she would invite me to her church. And of course I'd be glad to go.

I had started packing and deciding to whom I would give away household goods when Rosa Guy telephoned me from New York. She was my friend from the Harlem Writers Guild, and she had finished her book *Bird at My Window*. She wanted to come to California and promote it. I told her that if she could come soon, I would arrange a book signing and introduce her to bookstore owners. One week later Rosa arrived in Los Angeles wearing her New York air as casually as a well-worn cape that fitted her perfectly. She told me how all our New York City friends were faring, and the conversation made me think more about that hard and demanding and most glamorous city in the world.

Her novel of a dysfunctional relationship between a mother and son was gripping and sold well at the black-owned Aquarian bookstore. She could take a California success story back to New York.

Rosa was delighted when I told her that I was planning to return to New York. "Certainly, come to New York, you can stay with me. I have a big apartment uptown."

Abbey Lincoln and Max Roach had moved from Columbus Avenue to Central Park West. Their new apartment had an extra room. Abbey offered it to me over the telephone. Now I had two places I could stay.

Couples rarely know how much their togetherness shuts others out, and even if they did, there would be nothing they could do, save make everyone painfully self-conscious.

Rosa always had a string of devoted gentlemen friends, but since I had known her, she had not been the other half in a double arrangement—which seemed to say "We are together and you, third person, are invisible most of the time."

I accepted Rosa's offer and continued packing.

Everything said about the capricious nature of life and the best-laid plans is patently true. Just as I chose a departure date, my doorbell rang. When I opened the door, Bailey stood on the landing, his face grave.

"Baby, Guy returned to San Francisco three days ago, and I've come for you. He's in the hospital. He is in serious condition but not a life-threatening one. Get what you need." Surprise, whether good or bad, can have a profound effect on the body. Some people faint, some cry aloud. Bailey caught me as my knees buckled. He helped me back in the room to a chair.

Rosa asked what happened.

Bailey said, "Guy was sitting in a parked car that was hit by an out-of-control truck. Mother wanted to telephone you and tell you to fly up to San Francisco. I said no, that I would drive down and get you." He turned to Rosa. "Do you want to come with us, or will you wait till Maya gets back?"

Rosa said she was already packed and could fly home out of San Francisco as easily as out of Los Angeles. She would come with us.

In a few ragged minutes we were walking to Bailey's car. He handed me his car keys. "You drive."

"No, you know me. I might fall asleep."

"I drove all night to get here. Take the keys. You have me and your good friend in the car and you are trying to get to your son. Just remember."

I took the keys.

My passengers never awakened even when I stopped for gas.

Seven hours later I parked in front of Mother's house in San Francisco, and they woke up as if by plan.

Mother was waiting.

"He is stable. I've been talking to the doctors." She showed Rosa to a guest room and encouraged her to get some rest, adding that we would return soon. Mother drove her large car to the hospital.

Guy was ashen and looked like a grown man in the hospital bed. He was awake.

"Hello, my son."

"Hello, Mom."

He was stiff in our embrace. "I can't move much. My neck. It's broken again."

Suddenly I felt guilty. I had not been in the truck that hit him. In fact, I was not even in the same city where the accident occurred, and yet I felt guilty.

When something goes wrong with offspring, inevitably the parent feels guilty. As if some stone that needed turning had been left unturned. In the case of a physical handicap, the mother feels that when her body was building the infant, it shirked its responsibility somewhere.

I stood looking at my son, wondering where I had failed. I knew I would stay near until he recovered. I also knew that staying around Vivian Baxter would be strengthening.

She had a litany of morale-building sayings. "Keep your eyes on the road, your hand on the plow, your finger in the dike, your shoulder to the wheel, and push like hell." My mother would issue the statements as if from the godhead, and it was up to the hearer to fathom the meaning.

After a few days, Rosa left San Francisco for New York.

I visited Guy every day and watched as he slowly revived. I was right in my earlier observation. He was a grown-up stranger who reminded me of my son.

He said the University of Ghana had given him all it had to give. No, he wasn't sorry to leave Ghana, and although he had made some enemies, he had also made some friends he would keep for his lifetime.

As soon as he was well, he'd find work. Of course he would. He had had his first job at thirteen as a stacking boy in a Brooklyn bakery.

He would stay with his grandmother when he was released from the hospital. She would give him a roomful of her aphorisms. "Take care of your own business. Everybody else's business will not be your business." "Look to the hills from whence cometh your help." "You can tell a person by the company he keeps." "Never let your right hand know what your left hand is doing." Always adding that "each tub must sit on its own bottom."

I left San Francisco when I saw Guy sitting up like a golden prince and being served like a king in my mother's house.

Sixteen

Leaving Los Angeles was harder than I expected.

Human beings are like some plants. If we pause a few seconds in our journey, we begin setting down roots, tendrils that entangle other people as we ourselves are entangled.

Don Martin and Jimmy Truitt of the Lester Horton Dance School had been especially kind to me. When I took classes with them, they were careful not to let me appear ungainly, although I was fifteen years older than the other students. They deserved the courtesy of a farewell.

I was indebted to the Tee Oh Bee people as well as to Seymour Lazar, a Hollywood lawyer who had been generous with his advice and who gave me a nearly new car when mine refused to run another mile.

M. J. Hewitt had returned copper-colored from her South American trip and was full of stories I longed to hear. My friend Ketty Lester, a nightclub entertainer who sang as if she had a wind chime in her mouth, had to receive a good-bye.

I asked the help of Frances, Nichelle and Beah, and together we gave me a going-away party that spilled out of my house into Beah's, then into the big backyard, where ripe figs from a huge tree made walking messy.

I looked at Los Angeles anew and saw the fun I was having. I thought that leaving the town just as I was beginning to appreciate it might not be the best idea I had ever had. Then I remembered another of Vivian Baxter's truisms: "Take as much time as you need to make up your mind, but once it is made up, step out on your decision like it's something you want."

After I had survived the ugly rebellious years of "What can she possibly know that I don't?" I had followed my mother's advice to the letter and had not found her in error even once. I telephoned Guy to ask, "Are you going to be all right?" His tone was sincerely tender. "Mom, stop worrying. I'm your son and I'm a man."

When I pulled together the money I had been saving, it proved enough to get me to New York and keep me for at least two months. I'd have a job by that time.

Seventeen

Rosa's Upper West Side apartment was luxurious. The rooms were large and the ceilings so high that the place reminded me of the Victorian houses of San Francisco. The furniture was comfortable and the kitchen extraordinary, with the huge pots and outsize pans of a serious cook who was also a dedicated party giver.

People loved Rosa's parties for the food and her ability to make each person feel that with her or his arrival, the party could begin.

We quickly agreed that I would share expenses and cooking as long as I was there but that I would be looking with focused attention for my own apartment.

I had been in New York less than a week when Rosa decided to give a party. I asked if I could invite Dolly McPherson. Since she was an elderly woman, I wanted to ask her for around seven-thirty.

"Your friends won't be coming till around nine or ten. We'll have a drink and then she can get home before it's too late."

Rosa said that was all right with her.

African friends from the United Nations kept Rosa's liquor cabinet filled with a full complement of the most desired spirits, but she always insisted on buying her own wines. I was assisting with the cooking of banquet dishes when the doorbell rang.

I said to Rosa, "That must be Miss McPherson."

I had only to open the door to see how wrong I was. A beautiful young dark-brown-skinned woman wearing a lime-green dress stood before me.

Maybe one of Rosa's early guests. I said, "Good evening."

She said, "I am here to see Miss Angelou."

I said, "I am Miss Angelou."

She said, "You can't be. I mean, I am here to see the older Miss Angelou, maybe your mother."

I said, "I am the only Miss Angelou here."

We stared at each other for a few seconds.

I asked, "Are you Miss McPherson?"

She nodded, and we started to laugh at the same time.

She said, "The old goat."

We were still laughing when we sat down in the living room.

She asked, "What did he tell you about me?" I told her that the African had said she was an old but very intelligent woman who had been helpful to him.

"He could rightly say that. He courted me seriously and spent quite a few nights at my apartment."

It was my turn to say, "The old goat. And what did he tell you about me?"

"That you were very old and that you owned a house where you let rooms. He said you were one of those African–Americans who felt they had found something in Ghana, and you always had a soft spot for Africans in general and Ghanaians in particular."

Now I wanted to use a word more descriptive of the African than "goat," but the situation seemed so funny to me, and to Dolly as well, that even over drinks and throughout the party, whenever I caught her eye, we were both rendered speechless by laughter. We were both intelligent women who had been had by the same man. In more ways than one.

Eighteen

I knew there would be no peace for me until I visited the Audubon Ballroom. Until I let the grisly scene play out in front of me.

The dance hall and theater had been famous for decades. When I had gone visiting in the fifties, I often imagined Langston Hughes and Arna Bontemps and Zora Neale Hurston dancing the Charleston to the big-band music of Jimmy Lunceford, Count Basie and Duke Ellington.

Time passed and took away the popularity of orchestra music, the big bands and public dancing. When I went on my nostalgic walk to the ballroom in 1967, New York City had begun the process of condemning the Audubon.

Its meager reserve was realized from renting the premises to organizations, conventions, councils and committees.

On February 21, 1965, the Organization of African-American Unity had rented the ballroom for a fund-raiser. Malcolm X had been the speaker.

I approached the building slowly. The windows were dusty and the doors barred. As I tried to peer into the vast emptiness, the questions that crouched just beyond my conscious mind came full force.

Had I stayed in New York when I returned from Ghana, would I have been sitting with Betty Shabazz and her children?

Would I have heard the final words of Malcolm X?

Would I have heard the shots puncture the air?

Would I have seen the killers' faces and had them etched in my mind eternally?

I could see no shadow inside; no chimera arose and danced.

I walked away.

Nineteen

I had sung in Jerry Purcell's swank supper club once, and although I was not looking for nightclub work, I telephoned him. He invited me for dinner. We had been good friends, and I thought he might have some idea where I could find work. We met at his Italian restaurant, the Paparazzi.

He was still a big, movie-star-handsome man who walked as if he were heavier from his waist down than from his waist up. We greeted each other as old friends. I told him I was staying with a friend and that I was still writing poetry, but I longed to write plays and my money was disappearing faster than I had expected.

At that moment Jerry began to grow angel's wings. He said, "I'm in management now, and I am doing well."

He rose often from the table to greet customers and to speak to his staff, but he always returned, smiling. He was more affable than I remembered.

I said good-bye after lunch, and he handed me an envelope, saying that his office number and the name of his personal secretary were enclosed. He said I should find my own apartment and that if I needed anything, I should phone his secretary. He said, "Bring your friends here. Whenever. Just take the bill, add your tip and sign it."

He sent a waiter with me to hail a taxi. I sat back in the seat and opened the envelope. The number and the secretary's name were there, along with a large amount of cash.

For the next two years Purcell treated me like a valued employee. Save for the odd temporary office job and the money I made writing radio spots for Ruby Dee and Ossie Davis, I depended upon his largesse. He didn't once ask anything and seemed totally satisfied with a simple thanks. I did write a ballad based on *Portnoy's Complaint* for a singer Jerry managed. And I wrote twelve astrological liner notes for a series of long–playing albums he was planning to release.

When I tried to explain how his generosity afforded me the opportunity to improve my writing skills, he shrugged his shoulders and said, "I manage artists who make more in one night than you have ever made in a year. Yet I know no one more talented than you."

His patronage was a gift as welcome as found money bearing no type of identification.

Twenty

New York was vigorous, and its inhabitants moved quickly. Everyone was always going somewhere determinedly. There seemed to be no question or doubt about their destination. New Yorkers knew they were going to arrive, and no one had better get in the way.

In order to join New York's ebb and flow, I had to spend some time listening to the sounds, watching the streams of people coursing east and west and north and south. When I thought I had my balance, I dared to look for an apartment.

There are only so many times in life when our good fortunes and bad fortunes intersect. At such junctions, it is wise to pray, and failing that, keep the passport up-to-date and have some cash available.

The first few days, the city seemed an ice rink, and I was a novice wobbling on weak ankles. I continued going out each day to follow up on tips and hunt down newspaper listings.

I had wanted a flat in a brownstone, or at least a large apartment in one of the older buildings on Riverside Drive. Life offered me a one-bedroom apartment in a brand-new building on Central Park West. It was painted white, and its best feature was a long living room with big windows and a view of the park.

The place was clinical and so different from what I wanted that I thought bad fortune had caught me and I would be forced to live, at least for a while, in a cold and sterile environment. But life proved itself right and me wrong. Friends began giving me fine things for the apartment.

I was having dinner in a Harlem restaurant when a good-looking amber-colored man introduced himself. That is how I met the handsome Sam Floyd, who had the airs of a meticulous fop and the mind of an analytical scientist. He was one of James Baldwin's closest friends and, after a few months, became a close friend to me. His quick but never cruel wit lifted my spirits on many lean and mean days. I invited him to my empty apartment. He said, "People think New Yorkers are cold, but that is only when they are prevented from helping people who really don't need help. I have a small rug for you." We laughed. After we discovered that we really liked each other, we spent time together at least once a week.

Sam was only partially right. As soon as it became known that I had an empty apartment, I began to receive good and even great furniture. A desk came from Sylvia Boone, who had just returned from Ghana. The composer Irving Burgee, who had written calypso songs for Harry Belafonte, was the most financially successful member of the Harlem Writers Guild, and when he heard that I had a new apartment, he gave me a sleek table and an uphol-stered chair.

Twenty-one

Dolly McPherson and I were becoming good friends. Obviously we never revealed to anyone how we met. Either or both of us could have taken umbrage, and perhaps we did privately. But there was no reason to be angry with each other. Dolly had no way of knowing that when the man was with me, he acted as if he were my husband. And I couldn't know that when he wasn't with me, I aged about forty years and became an old black American lady who let rooms.

Dolly and I liked each other's ability to laugh at a circumstance that neither of us could undo. I met her family. Dolly's youngest brother, Stephen, looked so much like Bailey that I could hardly speak when we met.

Stephen was my brother's height and skin color, and was a brilliant research scientist. Like Bailey, Stephen had the wit to make me laugh at the most inane jokes and even at inappropriate times.

I wrote to Mother, "You didn't give me a sister but I found one for myself. As soon as possible I want you to come to New York and meet her."

Dolly and I started spending time in an antiques shop on the Upper West Side.

Bea Grimes had the only black-owned secondhand store on Broadway. I liked that she was a big country woman with a colorful vocabulary and her own business. She thought of me as being a lot like her, except I had a little more learning and owned practically nothing.

She and Dolly and I often sat talking in the musty crowded back of her shop. She found out that I hardly knew the difference between a Meissen cup and a Mason jar, but she did, and sitting in the gloom, often with a drink in a paper cup, she schooled me on what to look for in ceramics, china, and silver.

"What kind of silver you got?"

I told her that I had no silver.

"No silver? No silver?"

"My mother has silver. I'll be forty on my next birthday. It's too early for me."

Bea clucked her tongue and shook her head. "You ought to have bought yourself something silver on your thirtieth birthday. Even a silver spoon. You can't be a lady with no silver." She asked, "What you got sitting on your buffet?"

I hesitated.

Dolly said, "Oh, Bea, she doesn't have a buffet."

"Child, I'd better come around and see your place. I'm going to get you set up. You need some help."

Bea sold me an Eames chair for thirty dollars and a nineteenth-century Empire sofa for a hundred.

Bea needed to be needed and in fact liked the needing. She sat in that miasmic atmosphere surrounded by goods that had belonged to someone else who must have found pleasure in preserving them, might have even doted on them. Now they were abandoned to the often careless fingers of customers whose greatest interest was in haggling with the store owner to get a bargain price.

"These young white kids nearly give away their parents' and grandparents' things. You want to see something? Someday I'll take you to an estate sale. The heirs act like they don't care how much money they get. Main thing to them is get rid of this old stuff. Make you think seriously about dying, don't it?"

Thanks to Bea Grimes in particular and a host of friends in general, I was able to turn the clinical-looking apartment into a lush experience. Pale lilac silk drapes at the window, a purple wool sofa, one new pale green Karastan rug from Stern's, a reputable record player and I was ready to show off my home.

The Harlem Writers Guild members, along with Sam Floyd, James Baldwin, Connie Sutton and her husband, Sam, and the artist Joan Sandler, came to party. In fact, Jimmy's whole family came to party.

When I looked around, there were over fifty people in my suddenly small apartment, and they were having a New York good time. James Baldwin and Julian Mayfield and Paule Marshall were discussing the political responsibilities of writers. John Killens, the founder of the Harlem Writers Workshop, waded in with Alexander Pushkin. Ivan Dixon, the screen actor, on a visit from California, and M. J. Hewitt were sitting on the floor near the piano in deep conversation while Patty Bone, who had been Billie Holiday's accompanist, played a Thelonious Monk tune.

Sam Floyd and Helen Baldwin, Jimmy's sister-in-law, helped me in the kitchen. I used the make-do tip that my mother had taught me: "If more people come than expected, just put a little more water in the soup." She believed it was all right to turn away people for cocktails but bad luck to turn anyone away from a dinner party.

The party finally wound down and released its hold on the revelers. The food had been enjoyed and the drink had been served generously, yet there were leftovers sufficient for the next day's dinner and no one faced the grayness of dawn totally besotted.

Twenty-two

Jimmy Baldwin was a whirlwind who stirred everything and everybody. He lived at a dizzying pace and I loved spinning with him. Once, after we had spent an afternoon talking and drinking with a group of white writers in a downtown bar, he said he liked that I could hold my liquor and my positions. He was pleased that I could defend Edgar Allan Poe and ask serious questions about Willa Cather.

The car let us out on Seventy-first Street and Columbus Avenue, but I lived on Ninety-seventh and Central Park West. I said, "I thought you were taking me home." He said, "I am, to my home."

He started calling as he unlocked the front door. "Momma, Paula, Gloria, Momma?"

"James, stop that hollering. Here I am." The little lady with an extremely soft voice appeared, smiling. She looked amazingly like Jimmy. He embraced her.

"Momma. I'm bringing you something you really don't need, another daughter. This is Maya."

Berdis Baldwin had nine children, yet she smiled at me as if she had been eagerly awaiting the tenth.

"You're a precious thing, yes you are. Are you hungry? Let Mother fix you something."

Jimmy said, "I'll make us a drink. We won't be staying long."

Mother said, "You never stay long anywhere."

Their love for each other was like a throb in the air. Jimmy was her first child, and he and his brothers and sisters kept their mother in an adoring family embrace.

When we reached the door, I said, "Thank you, Mrs. Baldwin."

She asked, "Didn't you hear your brother? He gave you to me. I am your mother Baldwin."

"Yes, Mother Baldwin, thank you." I had to bend nearly half my height to kiss her cheek.

Twenty-three

I was job hunting persistently. Gloria, Jimmy Baldwin's sister, had told me that Andrea Bullard, an editor at *Redbook*, had learned that a job was going to become available at the *Saturday Review* and the administrators would be looking for a black woman.

I applied for a position in editing. Norman Cousins talked to me, and on a Friday afternoon, he asked that I write précis of five major articles taken from international journals and bring them to him on Monday by noon.

I said I would, but I was so angry that Dolly's office could hardly hold me.

"Obviously he doesn't want me for the job. If in fact there's a job at all."

Dolly said, "But you have had an interview with Cousins. There must have been something."

I told her, "Maybe there was something about me he didn't like. Maybe I was too tall or too colored or too young or old—"

Dolly interrupted, "Suppose it's none of those things?"

"Dolly, when an employer sets an impossible task for a want-to-be employee, he does it so that he is freed from hiring that particular employee and yet can say he did try. 'I did . . . but I couldn't find anyone capable of doing the work.'"

Dolly said, "You can do it, I know, and I'm going to help. Decide on the five journals and I'll ask my secretary to help over the weekend. We can't let this chance get away." She went on, "He's going to have to tell you to your face you are not what he wants." She began to move rapidly around her office, gathering papers.

I could hardly refute her statement. I knew I should never ask anyone to fight my battles more passionately than I. So I agreed to write the précis.

"International journals?" She called her secretary. "Mrs. Ford, I need five journals. Miss Angelou is going to do some research and writing tonight and tomorrow. I will also need your help on Sunday."

The secretary stood in the room, somber and contained.

"Intellectual journals from five countries. Thank you." Mrs. Ford left and returned with her arms filled. I was given *The Paris Review, The Bodleian, The Kenyan,* an Australian magazine and a German magazine.

The weekend was a flurry of encyclopedias and yellow pads. I sat on the floor with *Roget's Thesaurus*, the King James Bible and several dictionaries.

On Sunday, Mrs. Ford came to Dolly's apartment and typed my handwritten summaries. Dolly read them and declared, "This is as good as or better than anything they print in the darn magazine."

For Dolly, that was strong talk.

There are some people who are fastidious about the language they use, possibly because of their upbringing. Dolly and I could be alone in an empty apartment, yet if Dolly said "hell," she always spelled it.

Now she was still irate. She said, "If the editor had enough damned nerve to ask you for that much work in two days, you have enough damned nerve to write the pieces and deliver them in person before noon on Monday."

On Monday morning I stepped crisply into the office of the *Saturday Review.*

"I have an appointment with Mr. Cousins."

The receptionist said, hardly looking up, "He's not here."

"But I'm supposed to give him some digests. May I see his secretary?"

"She's not here, either. You can just leave them there."

She never once really looked at me, but I had the sensation that she had looked and seen right through me. At first glance, I appeared a nice-looking woman in her late thirties, well dressed, carefully coiffed, with more than enough confidence.

But the receptionist knew that I didn't belong there and she did. To her I was just another colored girl out of my place. Dangerously, her knowledge almost became my knowledge. I laid the pages on the desk and somehow got to the elevator as quickly as possible.

Twenty-four

Jimmy Baldwin had visited me the night before and our conversation had turned into a loud row. I was not surprised to hear his voice on the telephone.

"Hey, baby, are you busy?"

"Not too busy, why?"

"I'm coming to pick you up. I'll be in a taxi. I want to talk to you."

We didn't speak in the cab. The argument had been over the Black Panthers in general, of whom I approved, and Eldridge Cleaver in particular, who I thought was an opportunist and a batterer.

Jimmy had said, "You can't separate Cleaver from the Panthers. He is their general."

I had argued that Huey Newton was the general and Eldridge was a loudmouth foot soldier.

The Black Panthers had earned respect in the African-American community. They had started a school where the students were given free breakfasts and professional tutoring. They were courteous to women and addressed one another with kindness. Even the most archconservative privately admired their trim Panthers' uniforms topped by rakishly worn berets. The people were happy to see them stride through the neighborhood like conquering heroes accepting greetings.

Eldridge had a different air. It was as if he were years older than the others. When I saw him on television, he seemed more inimical and bitter than the other Panthers. They were angry, enraged and determined to do something about the entrenched racism, but he was aloof and chilly.

Jimmy had said, "Why are you skirting the issue? You don't like Cleaver because you don't like what he said about me."

"That's true. But that's not all."

"Yeah?" He had smiled, and his fine hands flew around in the air like dark birds. He knew me very well.

"You can't stand hearing anyone insult or even talk about your friends."

I had not responded. Not only was it true, I thought, but it was a good way to be.

When the cab stopped now on Forty-fourth Street, off Broadway, I asked, "We had to come to a transient hotel?"

He paid the driver. "It's sleazy, I know that, but I used to hang out here years ago. I come here a lot of times when I want to think." I was pleased that he would want me around while he thought.

It was early afternoon outside, but the dim bar and the reek of spilled beer and urine made me think of midnight in a low-down and dusty dive during prohibition.

Jimmy's eyes had no more time than mine to grow accustomed to the gloom, but he led me directly to the bar. Obviously he was familiar with the place.

He pulled out a stool. "Baby, you order drinks, I've got to make a phone call."

I ordered two Scotches and thought about the mind's whimsy. James Baldwin, whose writing challenged the most powerful country in the world, who had sat down with the president and who spoke French as if he had grown up on the streets of Montmartre, came to this dank dive to think.

I was absorbed in thought myself when a person moved too close to me.

"Hello. My name is Buck. Let me buy you a drink."

I looked up to see a huge man standing about an inch away from me.

I pulled back and said, "Thank you, but I'm with someone."

He grunted. "Well, he's not your husband."

"Oh really, how did you come to that conclusion?" I flinched a second after I asked the question. I really didn't want him to answer, in case his response would be too telling.

He stuck out his arm and shook his hand on a limp wrist. "He's one of those, you know."

"What I do know is that I am with him. So you'd better go to your seat before he comes back."

Jimmy did walk and gesture with feminine grace, but I couldn't allow the intruder to get away with his insinuations.

Buck was still talking when Jimmy returned. My eyes had grown used to the light given off by neon signs behind the bar. Jimmy saw the man, sized up the situation and neatly stepped between the offender and me.

He looked up into the intruder's face. "You've been looking after her for me, haven't you?"

Before Buck could answer, Jimmy said, "Thank you, you son of a bitch. Now you are dismissed."

Jimmy's ferocity shocked me, and my jaw dropped. It dropped farther when the man turned, unspeaking, and walked away.

Jimmy sipped his drink. "Well, baby, I'm going to California. I've decided that I should help Eldridge Cleaver."

Hearing his plans kept me speechless.

"I know you say you hate him, but he is a thinking black man, and he is in trouble because he is thinking and is talking about what he thinks. He needs our help."

I said, "Well, I thought about it, and what he wrote about your homosexuality in his stupid book was so vulgar that I'd rather hang him than help him."

"*Soul on Ice* is a very important book, and you have to remember, the son always kills the father."

The statement was intriguing. I mulled it over as Jimmy gathered his thoughts.

"I met Richard Wright in Paris and got to know him sufficiently," he said. "Everything about Wright that I disliked I wrote about in my essay 'Alas, Poor Richard.' Many Wright devotees were as angry with me then as you are now with Eldridge."

"I'm not a devotee." I hastened to put myself in a clearer light. "I love you, true, but I'm not a damned devotee. I am a careful reader, and I know the difference between your critical evaluation of Wright's post–*Black Boy* work and the hatchet job Cleaver did on you. Not on your work but on you, on your character."

"Maybe he couldn't find enough about my work to attack. Sometimes people assail the homosexual because they think that by flailing the gay boy, they can reduce that same tendency they suspect in themselves. It's difficult being different."

"Well, do you suppose if I know that, it will make it easier for me to see you go to California to help Cleaver?"

"Baby, understand when I say I am going to help Eldridge, and I hope I do, that I am really going for myself. Because it is the right thing for me to do. Understand?"

My own obstinacy would not allow me to concede quickly and admit that I did understand, and that I even hoped that if I found myself in the same or a similar circumstance, I would behave as wisely.

"Understand?"

More at that moment than ever before, he reminded me of Bailey. They were two small black men who were my big brothers.

I said, "I'm just afraid for you out there with those roughnecks."

"I am a roughneck, too. Grow up. Being black and my size on the streets of Harlem will make a choirboy a roughneck. But do you understand why I'm going?"

I said, "Yes."

Twenty-five

Jerry Purcell's East Side apartment was the epitome of elegance. I was invited to dinner, and I took Rosa with me. She marveled at the luxury and whispered, "And he's a bachelor?"

I told her, "Yes." Years earlier he had fallen for and married a movie starlet, but the marriage didn't last.

Jerry's partner, Paul Robinson, who was always at his side, was great company and could have been a professional comedian. Because he reproduced so accurately any accents relevant to his hilarious stories, he was irresistible.

I was pleased that Jerry was there to meet my friend and even more pleased that they seemed to like each other.

Jerry had sent out for food, and his housekeeper served us in the dining room.

Rosa came back from a trip to the bathroom. She whispered to me, "Girl, the faucets are gold."

I said, "Probably gold plate."

She lifted her shoulders and asked, "So?"

I saw her point. Anybody wealthy enough to have gold-plated bathroom fixtures was *wealthy*.

Jerry had asked me to bring some poems.

After I read them and received compliments, we played backgammon with much merriment. Jerry nodded at me. "Let me speak to you."

I followed him into a small sitting room.

"You're a good poet, and you might become great. You could become bigger than you imagine. Don't sell out, if I ever hear of you selling out . . ."

"How could I sell out? To whom would I sell out and what would I sell?"

"I mean, don't be stupid and use drugs."

I was flabbergasted. The night, which had been one of laughter and teasing, had turned into a drug-counseling session.

"There is no chance that I will ever use anything. I've learned a painful lesson from my brother."

"Okay. I had to say that. I've made a decision. I'm going to give you a monthly allowance. Continue working on your play and writing poetry."

He patted me on the back, and we returned to the living room. Amazement showed on my face.

Rosa asked, "Are you all right?"

I nodded. "It's probably time for us to go home."

Jerry turned to Paul. "Paul, will you drop Maya off when you go? Rosa's going to stay here a while. That's all right, Maya? If Paul takes you home?"

I looked at Rosa, who looked at Jerry, then back at me. She said, "I'll go with Maya," but the regret in her voice was palpable.

I couldn't get out of the apartment soon enough.

Paul Robinson said to Rosa, "He really fell for you. And you seemed to find him interesting."

Rosa said, "He's a nice man. I like him."

I asked, "But when did you know you liked him? I hardly heard you say two words to each other."

Rosa said, "I could be wrong, but I think I like him. No, I know I do."

There is a language learned in the womb that never

needs interpreters. It is a frictional electricity that runs between people. It carries the pertinent information without words.

Its meanings are "I find you incredibly attractive. I can hardly keep my hands off your body.

"And I am crazy to touch you, to kiss your mouth, your eyes."

The couple may have been introduced in a cathedral or a temple, but these are among the luscious thoughts each body sends to the other.

Some folks are born with more of that idiom than others. My body has always been slow-witted when it comes to that language. It neither speaks it fluently nor comprehends it clearly.

Twenty-six

The African was back. He telephoned from Ghana.

"I am not coming for you this time. You had your chances. Many chances. Now I am convinced that you do not love Africa. You do not love Ghana. I am not coming for you. I am coming to teach at one of your important universities. But I will bring you something. You are so American now. Would you like a car?"

His voice was so loud, he hardly needed a telephone.

I asked, "Why would you bring a car from Ghana? I'm living in New York. That is just down the street from Detroit. That's where they make cars."

"Maya, your tongue is too sharp, I've told you time and time again. You must watch out for your tongue."

But my tongue was all I had, all I had ever had. He had the stature, the money, his country, his sex, and now he was coming to my country to teach in an "important university" where I had never been. When it came to parrying, he had his armament, but I also had my weapon.

"I shall stay with the second secretary, who has a place near the United Nations, but I'd like to see you. Just for two hours. I'd like to invite some people I've not seen since my last visit." (I doubted that Dolly would be among the group.)

"How many should I prepare for?"

"Few. I think about ten."

That meant at least twenty.

"I'd be pleased to have them in my place."

"Then it's done. My host will bring me, so I suppose that makes us twelve. You can accommodate twelve?"

"Well, of course, when are you planning to come?" I expected to hear him say within the next month or so.

He said, "I'm traveling tomorrow. I'll spend a day in the U.K. and I'll be in New York on Friday. Can you see me then?"

"Um, yes. Yes. Of course." There would be time.

"Around three?"

"Three is fine."

A smile slowly moved across my face. I hugged myself with delight and telephoned Dolly.

We splurged on a bottle of good Spanish sherry and sat in her living room.

She said, "Of course he would never imagine that we'd meet."

I told her, "He's coming with some diplomats. We shall have to be careful."

She said, "I know you don't want to embarrass him."

"I certainly do want to embarrass him, but to himself, not to others."

Dolly grinned. I said, "I don't want to put his whole business in the street, but I have to get him back for 'She is an old American Negro who lets rooms . . .'"

Dolly said, "What about 'She is very, very old but very intelligent,' after whispering in my ear that I was very beautiful and that I had the skin of a young country girl?"

"He said that?"

"Many times."

"Oh, we must make him sweat, if only for a minute. He's got to sweat."

Our plans were concluded among peals of laughter and squeals of satisfaction, and for the next few days we had broad smirks on our faces.

Jimmy and Sam Floyd came for drinks.

Jimmy asked, "What's going on? You are the veritable cat who has lured the canary into its gullet."

"All I can tell you is it's not an innocent, hopeless, defenseless canary. If anything, I may be the house cat who plans to swallow down the lion."

"Be careful, baby. Learn from nature. How many times have you seen or heard of a tabby bearding a lion in its den?"

"I have not heard that, but I have heard of a pussy that dared to look at a queen."

My answer caught him, and he laughed loudly. "Okay. Okay. I still say be careful, baby, and let me know how it turns out."

Sam Floyd enjoyed the repartee with Jimmy. He laughed his little-boy coughing laugh and lit another Gauloise.

"That was quick and good, but I'm with Jim. Be careful. A big cat isn't swallowed down easily, and it can turn awfully fast. It's known for that."

I advised Dolly to put her clock in her purse (she never wore a watch) because we had to time her entrance to the minute. Drinks and groceries had to be bought and food had to be prepared.

In African homes and most African-American homes, the host expects, and is expected, to offer food and beverage to guests. The provisions may be as meager as a piece of fruit and a glass of water, but they must be offered.

The sight of him at my door made me lean against the jamb. He was as beautiful as ever and as black as ever. His skin shone as if it had just been polished, and his teeth were as white as long-grain rice.

Seeing me had some effect on him, too, for he rocked back and forth a few times before he entered the apartment.

We embraced but held ourselves in check. There were too many hard words like shields across our chests, and his escort entered close behind him and stood silent as we greeted each other.

I brought out schnapps, and although I expected it, I flinched when the African poured a few drops for the elders onto my Karastan rug.

We spoke of old friends and new woes. He had not gone to Guinea, where President Nkrumah lived in exile. He said lies and gossip and rumors filled the papers and radio reports. There had been an intimation that he supported the rebels who overthrew President Nkrumah.

"Maya, you yourself know that to be a lie. I was in Mexico with Kwesi Brew when the coup took place. And even so, I was always a Nkrumaist. They called me a verandah boy, meaning one who stood on the verandah talking about independence and then worked to kick the colonials out of our country. We were among the group who brought him to power."

I couldn't imagine anyone ever calling him a boy, even when he was twelve years old.

The doorbell rang, and in minutes my living room was furnished with people in rich robes and colorful caftans. Different languages sang in the air. I poured drinks, and although I had a pot of chili and rice, the company was satisfied with the fruit and cheese spread on the buffet next to the silver.

At exactly five minutes to four, while the company was engrossed in the African's conversation, I quietly went to the door and unlocked it. I picked up a glass of wine and went back to my seat.

At one minute to four, I interrupted the African. "Excuse me, but I and the other women here have a burning question I have been meaning to ask. I know you can answer."

He obligingly turned to me.

"Will you speak of fidelity? Is the African man more faithful than the European man? And what makes him so?"

He cleared his throat and spoke. "Yes, that is a lady's question, but having said that, it still deserves being answered." I might have kicked him had I not tasted the promised revenge on my tongue.

"The African man is more faithful than the European, not because he loves his woman more than the European loves his woman but because he loves himself more than the European man loves himself."

Dolly walked in the door. Only a few heads turned.

"You see, the African man is supposed to know where he is at all times. If he is in the wrong place, he knows that, and he has to leave . . ."

Dolly walked up to his chair and laid a hand on his shoulder. "Hello there."

He turned and looked up. It took him a second to register her face and another to remember where he was. He looked at me. The first question was, Did I see her, too? The second was, Did I know who she was? Really? The third was, How did she get here?

Dolly said coyly, "Won't you stand for me?"

He bounded out of his chair like a man half his age.

"Miss McPherson? Of course it's Miss McPherson."

Dolly said, "You can still call me Dolly."

"Of course, Dolly." Although her appearance benumbed him, he was able to operate in the familiar. He made small, small talk until he could recover.

"How have you been? Of course you've heard about what is going on in my country."

The joke had gone on long enough. From Dolly's face, I learned that she, too, had lost her taste for it.

I said, "Dolly, come to the kitchen, please." To the African, I said, "If you will rejoin the guests, we'll be right back."

In the kitchen, Dolly laughed and said, "He didn't know what to do."

I said, "Or who to do it to." We both laughed.

She asked, "Do you think anyone had any idea?"

"Certainly not. You were a pretty woman greeting a handsome man you had known somewhere else." I added, "Known in the biblical sense."

She laughed. "Girl, you ought to be ashamed of yourself."

We had given the African at least five moments of unease, which satisfied our appetites, and no one but he had been the wiser.

"He's lucky you're not mean," Dolly said.

"I think I'm lucky he found you and not some easy lady in the local bucket of blood."

She asked, "Who's to say he didn't find her, too?"

"Girl, you ought to be ashamed of yourself."

Back in the living room, the African had finished regaling his subjects with stories of current goings-on in Africa. He was standing.

"Maya, I must be going. My host needs to go to an appointment, and I shall accompany him. Tomorrow I shall continue my journey to Connecticut. Thank you for this brief respite at your place. Miss McPherson, oh, Dolly,

you must tell me how you met. I'll come back to New York
if Miss Angelou invites me."

He pointed to my bedroom and said to me, "I shall
need just a second of your time. May we go in here?"

We walked in and I closed the door.

"Maya, you are in danger."

"What?"

"You have become someone else in New York. Someone I don't know."

"What do you mean?"

"Did I ever try to make you a laughingstock in my
country?"

"No, but most of the time you treated me as if I were
an empty-headed flunky."

"I may have been wrong, but at least I was being
myself. This setup here is beneath you. You have tried to
belittle me. That is beneath the Maya I know and still
love."

He turned and walked back into the living room, saying, just loud enough for me to hear, "Pale hands I loved
beside the Shalimar."

I had told him once that if I ever became so angry
with him that I wouldn't speak, he could whisper that line

of poetry written by Laurence Hope and I would melt into the palm of his hand.

In the living room he spoke in Fanti to the people: "Let us leave these ladies and go attend to our business."

He turned to me and said in English, "I am going now, Maya, God bless you."

I saw hurt and embarrassment in his face. I had meant to prick him, not to pierce him.

I responded with the Fanti departure phrase, "*Ko ne bra*," which means "Go and come," but I knew he would never come back again.

I looked at Dolly, who was looking as crestfallen as I felt.

"Well, sister, we couldn't swallow the big cat easily. He seems to have stuck in our throats."

She said, "Yes, I know."

Twenty-seven

It was 1968, and the site was Carnegie Hall. Ossie Davis was to be master of ceremonies, Pete Seeger would sing, James Baldwin would spear up the audience and Martin Luther King, Jr., would conclude the evening. The concert was planned to recognize the hundredth anniversary of the birth of W. E. B. Du Bois. The historian had died in Ghana five years earlier at the age of ninety-five.

Jimmy had taken a box for family and friends, so Sam Floyd and Dolly and I joined the Baldwins and the baritone Brock Peters and his wife, Deedee.

The occasion was serious, but the people were lighthearted as they glittered in the lobby of Carnegie Hall.

When Ossie Davis appeared onstage in a sleek tuxedo that fitted him everywhere, the audience was eager for him. Ossie glowed with grace and pleased the patrons with his easy wit. Next, Pete Seeger, the well-known folk-singer, arched his long, lean body around his guitar and sang:

"Where have all the flowers gone?
Long time passing . . ."

The crowd showed their appreciation by asking for an encore.

James Baldwin flew onto the stage, talking before he even reached the microphone. The audience expected his machine-gun ack–ack way of speaking. There were shouts of approval at the end of each sentence. He flailed at this country that he loved, explaining that it could do better and had better do better or he could prophesy with a sign, water now but fire next time. He spoke to and for the people as if they were his family and they loved him. His rashness tickled them and his eloquence stroked them.

Everyone in the hall waited out a long moment before

Ossie reappeared. As if by an agreed-upon signal, we all held our breath.

Ossie's voice was filled with joy and respect. He said simply, "Ladies and gentlemen, Reverend Dr. Martin Luther King."

And he was there, smiling, nodding, waving a hand, an average-size, average-looking, average black man upon whom hung the dreams of millions.

He waited a while as the throng quieted, and then his voice filled the hall, filled our ears, filled our hearts.

When he began, his passion slowly wound his audience into a nearly unbearable tautness. A dramatic orator, King lured us back to the nineteenth century and into the mind of a young man who had been born black only a few years after the abolition of the slave trade, yet whose exquisite intelligence and courage allowed him to become the first African-American to earn a doctorate from Harvard University in 1895.

Martin King could have been describing a contemporary, or a relative, he spoke so knowingly of W. E. B. Du Bois. We listeners bonded resolutely, because King showed us how we were all related to one another and that we shared the same demons and the same divines. He cemented the bonding by telling us that Du Bois had included all of us, no matter our color, status or age, into his dream of a fair and workable future.

The melody in Martin King's speech changed subtly. Those familiar with the oratorical style of black preachers knew he had began his finale.

Mother Baldwin stretched out her legs, feeling for her shoes. Brock got up, as did Jimmy Baldwin and his brother David. I looked down on the main floor and was reminded of a black Baptist church on a Sunday morning when the preacher has told the parishioners the old story in a new way. Each time I looked, more people had risen, so that by the time Reverend King said his last word, everyone was standing.

The spontaneous response was tumultuous and the mood even more joyous than it had been in the early evening. Martin Luther King, Jr., never disappointed. The people had enjoyed the grace of Ossie Davis, the music of Pete Seeger, the excitement of James Baldwin. Then Martin King had held high his rainbow of good wishes for all the people, everywhere.

The Baldwin party was walking down the corridor from the box when Reverend King appeared.

Everyone complimented him. Mother Baldwin received a hug and praise for her son.

"I know you're proud of this fellow, aren't you, Mother?"

Berdis Baldwin blushed as if we were at Jimmy's christening and the preacher had declared her son to be the most wonderful child he had ever seen.

Martin King said to me, "And you, Maya. I wanted to talk to you. What are you doing now?"

I said I was writing a play.

"Can you put a bookmark on a page and give me one month of your time? This poor people's march we are girding up for is not a black march or a white march. This is the poor people's march. I want us to stay in Washington, D.C., until legislation is passed that will reduce the poverty in our rich country. We may have to build tent cities, and if so, I want to be able to do that."

"But what can I . . ."

More people had joined our group of Baldwins and friends.

"I need someone to travel this country and talk to black preachers. I'd like each big church to donate one Sunday's collection to the poor people's march. I need you, Maya. Not too many black preachers can resist a good-looking woman with a good idea."

Mother Baldwin said, "That's the truth."

Martin went on, "Also, when anyone accuses me of just being nonviolent, I can say, 'Well, I don't know. I've got Maya Angelou back with me.'"

Jimmy said, "Yes. Of course she will do it."

I saw, or thought I saw, how Reverend King was planning to expand the reach and influence of the Southern Christian Leadership Conference.

He asked for only one month. I said, "Yes, but only after my birthday. I have to give a party to explain to these hard-nosed New Yorkers why I'm going back to the SCLC. They think I'm much more of an activist, a real radical."

"What I'm planning is really radical. When is your birthday?"

I said, "April fourth."

We both nodded.

Twenty-eight

Guy had been Western Airlines' first black junior executive. He had declared he would keep the job for a specified time then go to Europe. His eighteen-month stay in the U.S. was up. He had bought a used Land Rover and was headed to London to pick it up. He had set aside one day to visit me in New York.

I decided to give a party and invite all the men who had advised and/or cautioned me when Guy was a rambunctious teenager. Since I was a single woman raising a black boy in the United States, I had asked a group of male friends to tell me when they thought I was treating Guy in a way that might endanger his sense of himself.

Many times after gatherings, I would receive phone calls. "Hey, Maya, Guy was playing chess and you made him leave the game. That wasn't hip."

"But it was just a game, and we had someplace to go."

"When a boy is playing a man, it's never just a game. It is about his manhood. He's always testing it."

Or: "You made Guy get up and give his seat to a woman. That wasn't hip."

"But it was courteous. I have to teach him courtesy."

"Yeah, but you didn't give him a chance to do the right thing on his own. You have to trust his upbringing."

I had listened and learned, and despite the past three or four rocky years, Guy had grown into a very nice young man. I wanted to show him off to my friends.

Coming from the supermarket I met Hercules, a freedom fighter from Rhodesia whom Guy and I had known in Cairo.

My mind was so filled with Guy's arrival that I didn't remember that in Cairo Hercules had tried to be Guy's buddy, and although I was married, he had attempted to seduce me.

Hercules asked how I was and how Guy was.

I told him Guy was in New York for just one day and that I was giving a party for him that night. I gave Hercules the address and told him he would be welcome.

When I entered the apartment, Guy had a wall-size map spread on the floor.

"Here, Mom, here's where I want to go."

It was the Sahara Desert.

I thought he was going back to Ghana, where we had friends.

"No, I'm going to have a photographic safari service from Mauritania back to Morocco."

My only child? My beloved son with whom I was now well pleased? My heart fell in my chest, but I said nothing. The red and green lines on the map seemed to be moving.

"I've planned it out with friends. We're going to meet up in Spain so we can run with the bulls in Pamplona, then we'll take this road to the Mediterranean and ferry over to Morocco."

He looked at me very quickly, as if he had been thinking aloud and suddenly remembered that I was present.

"Mom, you're afraid." It was not a question, he had read fear on my face.

"Yes. I am."

He said, "I understand, but you needn't be. I am free, and I have you to thank for that."

I didn't dare question; nor did I dare let him see my fear again. I asked him to help me put away the groceries and to second my cooking.

We fell into a rhythm that we had begun to develop when he was ten, except now he was adept. No onions went scooting across the floor, no fingers had to be washed, kissed and bandaged.

I admired the man, but I did miss the boy.

The party was merrily rolling along. Friends who hadn't seen one another in too long a time were having a reunion. I didn't know any young girls to invite as company for Guy, but Dolly asked over a new teacher who was on her first job. Guy came to the kitchen. "Mom." He was displeased. "Mom, Hercules is here."

The look on his face shook my memory loose. Of course, all the hosts in and around Cairo had stopped inviting Hercules. Housekeepers' young daughters were claiming they had been raped or impregnated by him, and since he had taken up drink, his language was often foul.

I shook my head and said to Guy, "I forgot. I was thinking about you and forgot."

He wagged his head and pitied his old doddering mother. I was thirty-nine.

I listened to the discussion between Jimmy Baldwin and Max Roach. They were talking about South Africa.

Hercules came up to me. "Sister Maya, thank you for inviting me."

I said "Yes" coolly.

He said, "I brought my girlfriend. Let me introduce her."

He introduced me to a woman standing at his side. I admit that my displeasure with myself, and the memory of Hercules's behavior in Egypt, kept me from acknowledging the guest warmly. I said a perfunctory hello and went to join another small group.

I was looking for a way to get into the heated discussion among John Killens and Julian Mayfield and Rosa Guy when Hercules's woman tugged my sleeve.

"Is it my whiteness that makes you uncomfortable?" She could not have startled me more if she had poured her drink on the rug.

I collected myself sufficiently. "Of course not. Look around, there are Sam and Connie Sutton, and Roger and

Jean Genoud. You are no more white than they, and they are at home here. Please, help yourself to a drink."

I moved to a less troublesome area and caught up on the laughter that was loud in the room.

Later, Dolly, Guy and I laid out the food on the buffet and the dining table. I stood with serving spoons in hand and said in a loud voice, "Grub est servi."

The line was taut and furiously fast at first, then, when it slackened, some people who had eaten jumped back in line for seconds.

I said, "Please, let everybody get served once before seconds are handed out."

Hercules's lady friend, who was back in line, said, "This is not the democratic way. First come, first served. Can you really hold a place in line for someone who is not here?"

I said, "Yes, I can. Because this is my house. I wouldn't tell you how to run it at your house."

Hercules said, in support of his lady, "She is right. This is not the democratic way."

My patience with them and with myself was as brittle as melba toast. I said, "You, who have needed a passbook to move from one district in Johannesburg to another, are to tell me about democracy?"

She said, "You people, you kill me. You don't realize that English is not his first language."

I was ready to evict her at "you people," but I was serving a plate. When I finished dishing up food, I said to Hercules, "Take her out of my house. She may be indulged and famous as a rude guest in other people's homes, but she gets put out of mine."

Suddenly the laughter had stopped, and all was quiet. I had not raised my voice, but I knew everyone present had heard me.

I couldn't take back a single word, and in that moment I hated myself and the woman. I sounded like a bully, and I truly abhorred bullies.

"Out." It was too late. "Out."

The woman's departing statement cut me more deeply than she could have ever imagined. "People think you're so kind. They should see you as you are. A great bully."

I said nothing, and in a few minutes, noise returned and the party pitch reestablished itself.

Guy left early to see the teacher home. Some friends said, "You showed wonderful restraint. She came out to be trouble."

Others didn't mention the incident. When I was totally alone, I sat down and wondered how else I could have handled that awful situation. I found no answer, so I started to clean the apartment. I emptied ashtrays and washed glasses. I took trash to the garbage chute. Little by little, I cleaned and polished my house till it glistened.

As I finished, Guy rang the bell. He entered and stood at the door, observing the clean apartment.

"I meant to be back in time to help you."

"Oh no, as you see . . ."

"Mom, I'm going to make us both a drink." I sat down to await the service.

He brought two filled glasses into the living room. He lifted his to me, I lifted mine to him.

"Mom, if you ever speak to a woman I bring to your house as you spoke to that woman, I will sever our relationship."

I looked at my son sitting aloof like a high-ranking judge on a lofty seat. His words alone constituted a body blow, and his posture added weight to the statement. I thought of carrying him on my hip all over the world, of sleeping in hotel rooms separated by a sheet hanging across the middle of the room to give each of us privacy. I thought of how I had raised him and saw that he was right.

I said, "Of course, you are absolutely correct. You are obliged to protect anyone you bring out anywhere. If the person is under your umbrella, you are supposed to defend her or him. It would kill me if you severed our relationship. But let me tell you this. If you bring someone to my house that stupid, it is likely that I will speak to her as I spoke to that woman. And severing our relationship will be your next job."

He looked at me for a long minute, then got up and came to the sofa to sit beside me.

He opened his long arms. "I love you, Mom, you're a gas. I truly love you."

Twenty-nine

John Patterson was my across-the-hall neighbor, and we shared the same birthday.

I spent the morning cooking for my party. He was planning to celebrate with his fiancée, a beautiful fawn-like girl half his age.

When I could safely leave my pots for a few minutes, I went to his apartment for a glass of wine and for our opportunity to congratulate each other.

I cheered him for his impending marriage, and he saluted me for taking on a thirty-day job that would give me the chance to visit the major American cities. I always added "and churches."

I didn't have my itinerary, but I told John that I thought I had to go to Atlanta first for meetings with Reverend King and the leaders of the SCLC.

I admitted to Dolly that I had trepidation about the trip, and even some fear over how the ministers in the different churches would take to me and to Reverend King's plans. So much depended upon my doing well.

Dolly said, "If the Reverend King thinks you can do it, that's enough for me. And don't believe that the whole thing depends on you. You're not the only fish in the sea. He's got others. Anyway, you will do wonderfully."

A sister always knows how to set you down, and a true sister lets you down easily.

My apartment smelled like I was readying for a Christmas feast. I was really putting on the dog. Stepping out. All the Harlem Writers Guild members were coming. I invited Jerry Purcell and his partner, Paul Robinson, and some of the regulars from Terry's Pub, the local bar.

I cooked Texas chili without the beans, baked ham and candied yams, rice and peas for the West Indian palate, macaroni and cheese and a pineapple upside-down cake.

I looked the apartment over and was proud. The food was prepared, ice buckets were filled, glasses were sparkling and the daffodils were as perky as their name.

The telephone ring surprised me.

"Maya?" It was Dolly.

"Yes?"

"Have you listened to the radio or television?"

I said no.

"Maya, please don't turn either of them on. And don't answer the phone. Give me your word."

"I give you my word."

"I'm on my way."

I made a drink and sat down, trying to guess what could have happened that could cause her such alarm.

Dolly stood at my door, her face ghastly with news.

I said, "Come in. Nothing could be that bad."

It was that bad and worse.

She said, "Martin Luther King was shot. Maya, he's dead."

Some words are spoken and not heard. Because the ears cannot accept them, the eye seems to see them. I saw the letters D E A D. Who was dead? Who was dead now?

Not Malcolm again. Not my grandmother again. Not my favorite uncle Tommy. Not again.

I didn't realize I was talking, but Dolly grabbed me and held me.

"Maya, it's Martin King. Reverend King."

"Stop talking nonsense. Stop it." When I really heard her, the world capsized. If King was dead, who was alive? Where would we go? What was next? Suddenly I had to get out.

I didn't take my purse or keys or turn off the stove or the lights or tell Dolly where I was going.

John was locking his door. We looked at each other.

He asked, "Where are you going?"

I said, "Harlem."

He said, "Me, too."

He didn't speak as we walked to Harlem. I turned my thoughts over as one turns pages in a book. In the silence I spoke to myself, using the time to comprehend the emptiness.

That great mind, which considered adversity and said, This too shall pass away, had itself passed away.

That mellifluous voice, which sang out of radios and televisions and over altars and pulpits, which intoned from picket lines and marches and through prison bars, was stilled. Forever stilled.

That strong heart, which did beat with the insistence of a kettle drum, was silent. Silenced.

Waves of noise of every kind flooded down 125th Street. There was an undulation of raw screams, followed by thuds like the sound of buffaloes running into each other at rutting time. I never discovered what or who caused that particular dissonance, but the sheer jangle of glass breaking was obvious.

When John ran into friends and they fell into a sob-bing embrace, I walked on alone.

There were noticeable differences between this cur-rent turmoil and the Watts uprising. In Los Angeles, rage had ruled. There, the people acted out of a pent-up anger over past slights and historic cruelties. On the evening of April 4, 1968, a lamentation would rise and hold tremu-lously in the air, then slowly fall out of hearing range just as another would ascend.

Strangers stopped in front of strangers and asked, "Why? Why?"

"You know? You know."

Then strangers hugged strangers and cried.

A television in the window of an appliance store played tapes of Martin King speaking. No sound accompanied the pictures, but people stood silent, five deep in front of the shop window, as the uproar swirled unnoticed around them. I joined the watchers for a few moments and heard the moan behind me.

Rosa Guy emerged from the crowd. We stood looking at each other. We embraced and said nothing. When we released each other, we continued our separate ways.

A man, naked to the waist, walked out of a building with a conga drum strapped to his body. He waddled toward me, the head of the drum protruding from under his arm. He passed me shouting, not singing, unintelligible words.

I went into a lighted diner and sat at the far end of the counter. Only one other customer was in the place. He was leaning over so far his head was on the counter.

I waited for a few minutes for a waitress, and when none appeared, I called out, "Can I get some service?"

The man raised his head. "If all you want is coffee, you can get it yourself."

I went behind the counter and lifted the coffeepot and looked at the man. "May I help you?"

"No, baby, nobody can help me. Nobody can help nobody. You know this is all about Malcolm."

"What?"

I expected to hear the awful despair at Martin Luther King's death. Malcolm's name shocked me.

"Malcolm?"

"See, they killed him not far from here, and we didn't do anything. Lot of people loved Malcolm, but we didn't show it, and now even people who didn't agree with Reverend King, they out here, just to show we do know how to care for somebody. Half of this is for Malcolm X, a half for Martin King and a half for a whole lot of others."

I laid my own head on the counter weighted with new realization.

A man lived. A man loved.

A man tried, and a man died.

And that was not all there was to that. And it never was.

Thirty

Death of a beloved flattens and dulls everything. Mountains and skyscrapers and grand ideas are brought down to eye level or below. Great loves and large hates no longer cast such huge shadows or span so broad a distance. Connections do not adhere so closely, and important events lose some of their glow.

Everywhere I turned, life was repeating itself. The photograph of Coretta Scott King, veiled and standing with her children, reminded me of the picture of Jacqueline Kennedy with her children. Both women were under the probing, curious and often sympathetic eye of the world. Yet each stood as if she and her children and her memories lived together in an unknowable dimension.

On radio and in newspapers, Martin King's name was linked again and again with the name Malcolm X. As if the life and death of one confirmed the life and death of the other.

Depression wound itself around me so securely I could barely walk, and didn't want to talk.

I went to Dolly's apartment. I didn't want my absence to alarm her.

"I'm going to hibernate for a few weeks."

She asked, "What do you mean?"

"I'm going to stay alone. I will not be seeing anyone. I just need to seek balance."

Dolly said, "I understand. But listen, I'm going to bring you some food. And you're going to have to talk to me once a day. I don't care what you say, just don't stop talking. Okay?"

Jerry Purcell sent an employee who knocked on my door loudly and repeatedly. When I opened it, he handed me a package wrapped in tinfoil.

"Jerry said that you would get a plate every other day. If you're not here, I'll leave it by the door."

Jimmy Baldwin pried me loose from my despair. "You have to get out of here. Get dressed. I'm taking you some-where."

Exactly what Bailey had said and done when Malcolm was killed.

"Put on something that makes you feel pretty." I remembered the old saying, which was a favorite of my Arkansas grandmother. "It's hard to make the prettiest clothes fit a miserable man."

Jimmy said, "Some friends have invited me to dinner, you will enjoy them. They are both funny, and you need to laugh." We were in front of the building before Jimmy said, "This is Jules Feiffer's apartment."

Judy opened the door and welcomed us. Although I had not formed a picture of the Feiffers, I was unprepared for her beauty. She could have been a movie actress. Jules also surprised me. He looked more like a young, intense college professor than one of the nation's funniest, most biting cartoonists.

They both hugged Jimmy, and the three of them laughed aloud as if they had heard a funny story when they last parted and had not had time to finish their laughter.

The Feiffers' pretty ten-year-old daughter joined us in the living room. When Jimmy embraced her and asked after her school, she answered easily, showing the poise of a person twice her age.

We adults finished our drinks and moved into the dining room. We told and heard great stories over a delicious dinner. Jimmy talked about being a preacher in Harlem at fourteen years old. He may have lost some of his evangelical drama, but it returned that night in force. He preached a little and sang in a remarkably beautiful voice. His story was funny and touching. When we laughed, it was always with him and with the people he spoke of, never at them.

Jules talked about school and his college mates. His tale was told with wit so dry that when we laughed, we thought we breathed in dust.

Judy kept the glasses filled and added the appropriate response whenever it was needed. She said, "Nothing funny ever happened to me until I met Jules."

When my time came, I thought of the saying "You have to fight for the right to play it good." I described Stamps, Arkansas. Although there is nothing amusing about racial discrimination, the oppressed find funny things to say about it.

"The white folks are so prejudiced in my town, a colored person is not allowed to eat vanilla ice cream.

"And when a white man heard a black man singing 'My Blue Heaven,' he called the KKK. They visited the offender and told him that the Molly in the lyric was a white woman, and they wanted to hear how he would sing the song now that he had new information."

I sang what the black man supposedly sang:

"Miss Molly and y'all
I ain't in that stuff at all
Y'alls happy in y'alls
Blue heaven."

There was very little serious conversation. The times were so solemn and the daily news so somber that we snatched mirth from unlikely places and gave servings of it to one another with both hands.

The evening was full. I was on the street before I realized how much I had relaxed in the Feiffers' home. I told Jimmy I was so glad to laugh.

Jimmy said, "We survived slavery. Think about that. Not because we were strong. The American Indians were strong, and they were on their own land. But they have not survived genocide. You know how we survived?"

I said nothing.

"We put surviving into our poems and into our songs. We put it into our folk tales. We danced surviving in Congo Square in New Orleans and put it in our pots when we cooked pinto beans. We wore surviving on our backs when we clothed ourselves in the colors of the rainbow. We were pulled down so low we could hardly lift our eyes, so we knew, if we wanted to survive, we had better lift our own spirits. So we laughed whenever we got the chance.

"Now, how does your spirit feel?"

I said, "Just fine, thank you."

Thirty-one

They were from Northern California and looked the part. Jon wore a loose-knit tan sweater with leather elbow patches and tan pants. Verna, a small, neatly made woman, sat comfortably in a light-colored Chanel suit, and Steve wore black slacks and a black V-neck sweater over a white turtleneck shirt that filled in the V.

They had gotten my address from Enrico Banducci, who owned the Hungry I in San Francisco. Enrico and I liked each other, so we had kept in touch over oceans and continents.

"Ms. Angelou, we know you are a writer and, we are told, a very good one."

"Yes."

"Do you have anything published?"

I didn't think it wise to say I had a short story published in *Revolución*, Cuba's premier magazine.

I said, "Ah." Then I added, "I have written some short essays that Ruby Dee and Ossie Davis read on a national radio station."

"We'd be glad to see them."

"Yes, they could tell us a lot about your style."

"When I heard you were looking for a writer, I put a few in my attaché case." I had borrowed the attaché case from Sam Floyd. "Please tell me what kind of writer are you looking for."

Jon leaned back and said, "We think it's past time for our station to do some programs on African-American culture and history. We were told that you have lived in Africa, and you might be the very person to bring it together for us."

Steve said, "We need an insider's view." Well, I certainly was inside.

"I am writing a play now, but I do have some ideas for a documentary."

"Would the subject of African–American culture be of interest to you?" Steve asked.

"Of course!"

Steve flinched. I did not intend to speak so abruptly, but the question was so inane it caught me off guard.

"Of course," I said more softly. "In fact, in Ghana I was struck by how much of what I thought was Afro-American culture really had its origin in Africa. Now I know I should have anticipated that, but I did not."

Jon asked, "Do you think you have enough material?"

"How long do you want the program?"

"No, no," Verna said, "not a program, we want a series. Ten one-hour programs. Can you do that?"

"Certainly. Surely. I just misunderstood. Ten one-hour programs?" I wondered if there was that much material in the whole world. "Yes. I can do that."

"We will be seeing other writers, but who is your agent?"

Would they even consider me if I admitted I had no agent?

"I have a manager. He acts as my agent." Having a manager might make me seem an important writer. "I'll give you his address and telephone number."

I wrote down Jerry Purcell's phone number. "He's away today, but I'm sure you can reach him tomorrow at this number."

I needed the day to find Jerry before they talked to him. I had to tell him that he was my manager.

For over an hour we talked about San Francisco and the state of the Broadway stage and PBS in general and their station KQED in particular and the United States and Africa. That was the kind of conversation I liked to have, rambling, tumbling, wandering off from one subject onto another.

Their humor pleased me. I forgot where I was and why I was there. When they stood, I remembered and immediately wondered if I had talked too much and overstayed my welcome. We shook hands all around, and Jon said, "We will speak to your manager, and you will hear from us before the week is out."

Yes, I did like them, and I hoped they liked me.

Three days later Jerry telephoned. "I got good money for you, so you'll be going out to San Francisco."

I whooped all the way to the library.

With time and a kindly librarian, any unskilled person can learn how to build a replica of the Taj Mahal. I pored over books about television documentaries. I read instructions on how to write television plays and accounts of producing and directing television.

I studied hard and memorized phrases and words I had never used. Boom and speed and camera angle, tripod and seconds and reverses. After a week I had an enlarged vocabulary. When I wasn't reading about television, I was writing for television.

I thought that I would learn on the job, but I would learn quicker and more easily if I had some of the language.

I designed a series called *Blacks. Blues. Black.* We were blacks in Africa before we were brought to America as slaves, where we created the blues, and now we were painfully and proudly returning to being upstanding free blacks again.

The program would show African culture's impact on the West. As host, I would introduce the lyricism of poetry and the imagery of prose. In one program I would have B. B. King playing blues and church choirs singing spirituals and gospel songs. There would be African, African-American and modern ballet dance, and I would point out their similarities. The art of African sculpture would be shown as the source and resource of many Western artists' creativity. I would place Fan, Ashanti and Dogon masks alongside the works of Picasso, Klee, Modigliani and Rouault.

It was thrilling to think of returning to San Francisco, with something to do and the faith that I would do a good job.

Thirty-two

I was so excited that the telephone call hardly penetrated.

"My name is Robert Loomis, and I am an editor at Random House. Judy Feiffer spoke of you. She said you told wonderful stories."

"How nice of her. James Baldwin and her husband told the best."

"I am calling to ask if you'd like to write an autobiography."

I said, "No, thank you. I am a poet and playwright."

He asked, "Are you sure?"

"Yes, quite. In fact, I'm leaving in a few days to write and host a television series for PBS in San Francisco. I'll be there for a month or more."

"May I have a California number for you?"

I gave him Aunt Lottie's San Francisco telephone number and my mother's number in Stockton, California, where she had moved.

"I'm pretty certain that I will not write an autobiography. I didn't celebrate it, but I have only had my fortieth birthday this year. Maybe in ten or twenty years." We both laughed and said good-bye.

In San Francisco I collected dancers and singers and musicians and comedians. I went to churches and synagogues and community centers. On the day of the first shoot, Bob Loomis telephoned again.

"Miss Angelou, I'm calling to see if you've had a change of mind, if you are certain that you don't want to write an autobiography for Random House."

I said, "Mr. Loomis, I am sure that I cannot write an autobiography. I am up to my lower jaw in this television series. When I come back to New York, I'd like to talk to you about a book of poetry."

He said, "Fine," but there was no eagerness in his voice. "Good luck to you."

.   .   .

In San Francisco I was pleased that all the pieces were falling into their proper places. The ministers I approached were agreeable, the choir conductors were talented and willing. I borrowed an entire collection of Makonde sculpture from Bishop Trevor Hoy at the Pacific School of Religion and church officials allowed me to film their services. I took television crews into elementary schools and people's private homes.

Blacks. Blues. Black was well received. The *Sun Times*, the local black newspaper, gave it a rousing review. Rosa Guy and Dolly came out for the premiere.

People who had looked askance when I began the series were now standing in line to participate. Schools had adopted the programs, and I was told that some preachers were using my subjects as topics for their sermons in San Francisco.

On my last day, Robert Loomis called again. I have always been sure that he spoke to James Baldwin. He said, "Miss Angelou, Robert Loomis. I won't bother you again. And I must say, you may be right not to attempt an autobiography, because it is nearly impossible to write autobiography as literature. Almost impossible."

I didn't think. I didn't have to. I said, "Well, maybe I will try it. I don't know how it will turn out, but I can try."

Grandmother Henderson's voice was in my ear: "Nothing beats a trial but a failure."

"Well, if you'd like to write forty or fifty pages and send them to me, we can see if I can get a contract for you. When do you think you can start?".

I said, "I'll start tomorrow."

Thirty-three

Rosa and Dolly and I traveled to Stockton to spend a last weekend with my mother before returning to New York.

She cooked and laughed and drank and told stories and generally pranced around her pretty house, proud of me, proud of herself, proud of Dolly and Rosa.

She said black women are so special. Few men of any color and even fewer white women can deal with how fabulous we are.

"Girls, I'm proud of you."

In the early morning, I took my yellow pad and ball-point pen and sat down at my mother's kitchen table.

I thought about black women and wondered how we got to be the way we were. In our country, white men were always in superior positions; after them came white women, then black men, then black women, who were historically on the bottom stratum.

How did it happen that we could nurse a nation of strangers, be maids to multitudes of people who scorned us, and still walk with some majesty and stand with a degree of pride?

I thought of human beings, as far back as I had read, of our deeds and didoes. According to some scientists, we were born to forever crawl in swamps, but for some not yet explained reason, we decided to stand erect and, despite gravity's pull and push, to remain standing. We, carnivorous beings, decided not to eat our brothers and sisters but to try to respect them. And further, to try to love them.

Some of us loved the martial songs, red blood flowing and the screams of the dying on battlefields.

And some naturally bellicose creatures decided to lay down our swords and shields and to try to study war no more.

Some of us heard the singing of angels, harmonies in a heavenly choir, or at least the music of the spheres.

We had come so far from where we started, and weren't nearly approaching where we had to be, but we were on the road to becoming better.

I thought if I wrote a book, I would have to examine the quality in the human spirit that continues to rise despite the slings and arrows of outrageous fortune.

Rise out of physical pain and the psychological cruelties.

Rise from being victims of rape and abuse and abandonment to the determination to be no victim of any kind.

Rise and be prepared to move on and ever on.

I remembered a children's poem from my mute days in Arkansas that seemed to say however low you perceive me now, I am headed for higher ground.

I wrote the first line in the book, which would become *I Know Why the Caged Bird Sings*.

"What you looking at me for. I didn't come to stay."

ABOUT THE AUTHOR

Poet, writer, performer, teacher and director MAYA ANGELOU was raised in Stamps, Arkansas, and then went to San Francisco. In addition to her bestselling autobiographies, beginning with *I Know Why the Caged Bird Sings*, she has also written five poetry collections, including *I Shall Not Be Moved* and *Shaker, Why Don't You Sing?*, as well as the celebrated poem "On the Pulse of Morning," which she read at the inauguration of President William Jefferson Clinton.